MAPALAKATA

ROBIN BERNSTEIN

MAPALAKATA

GOST

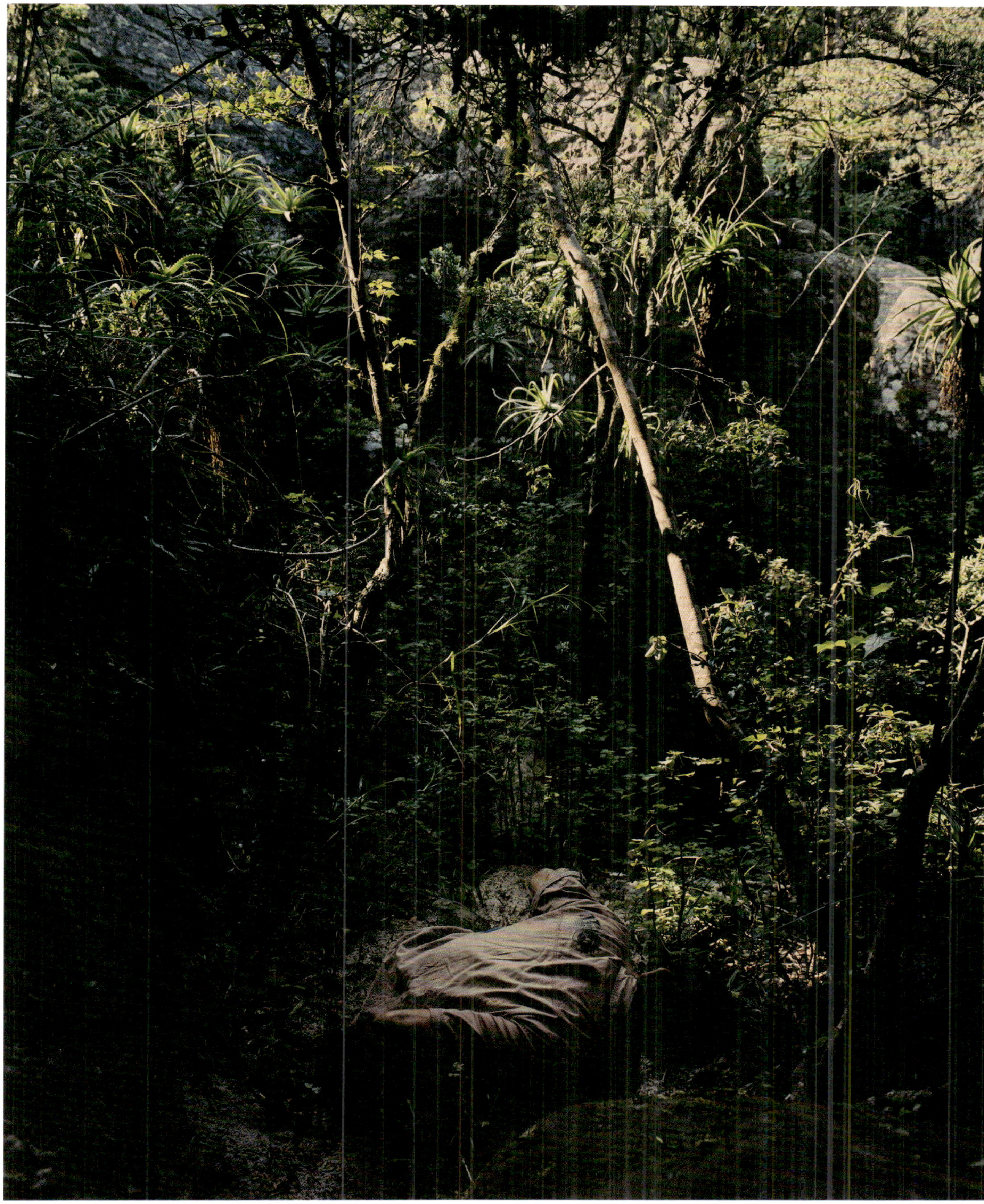

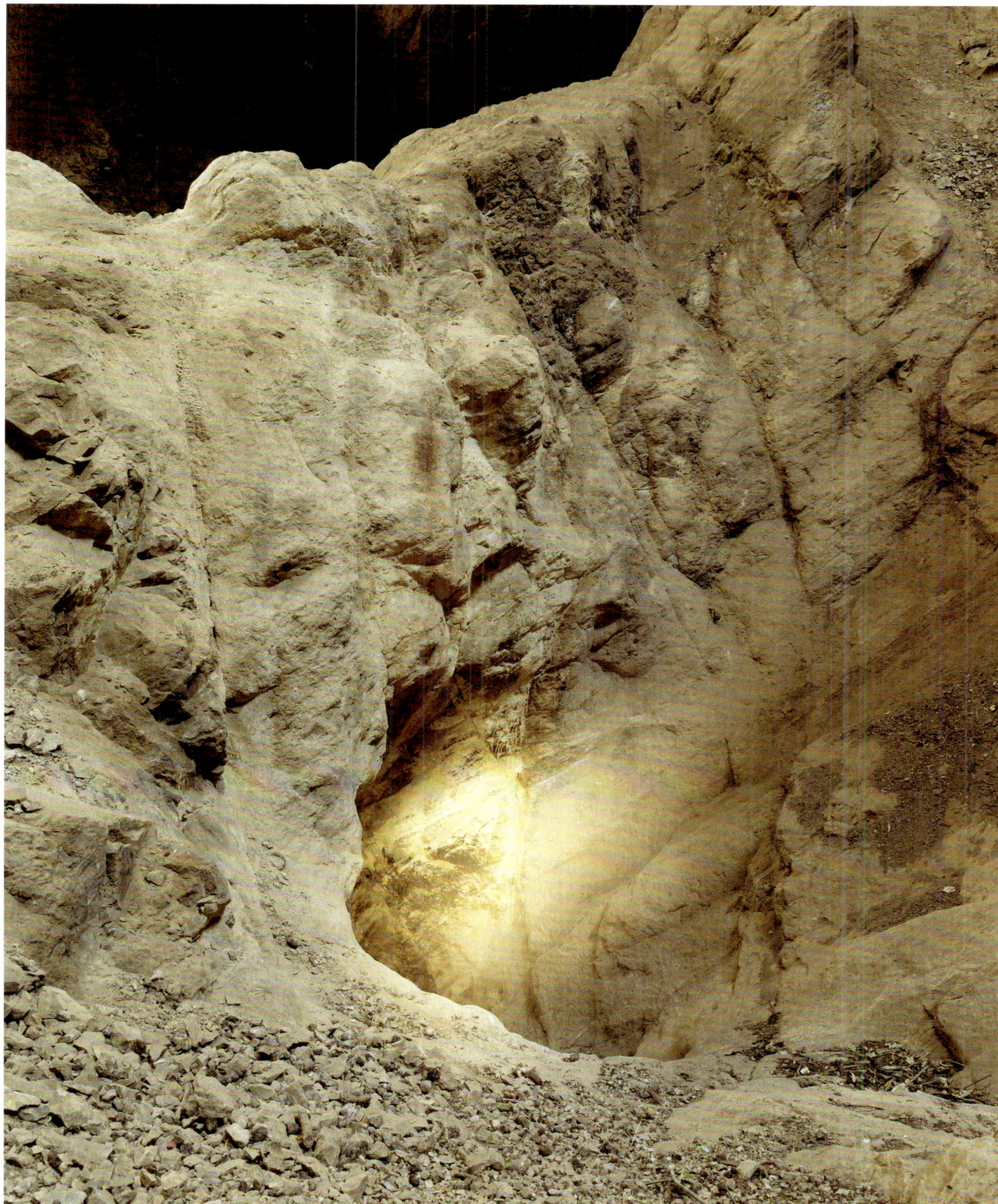

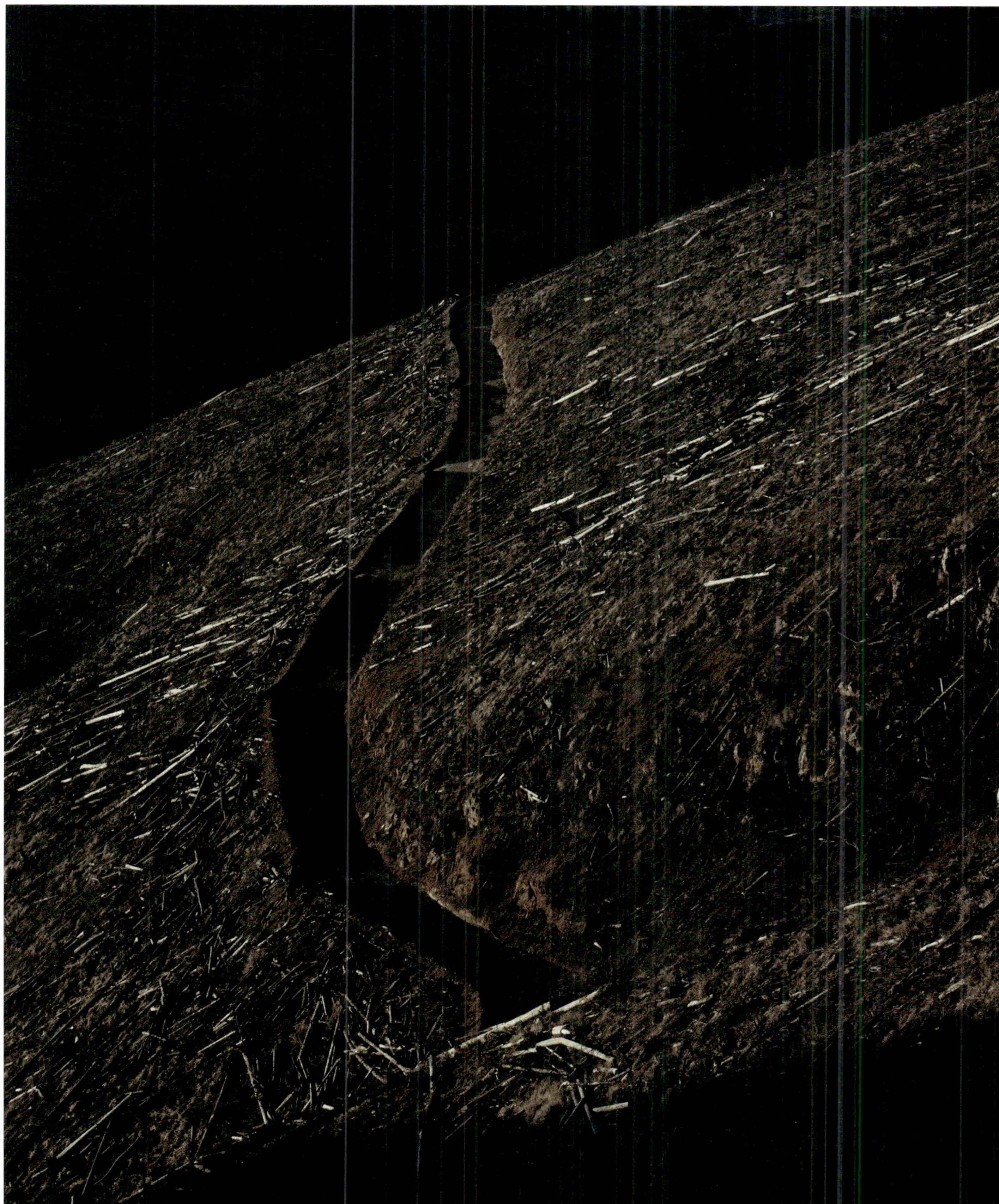

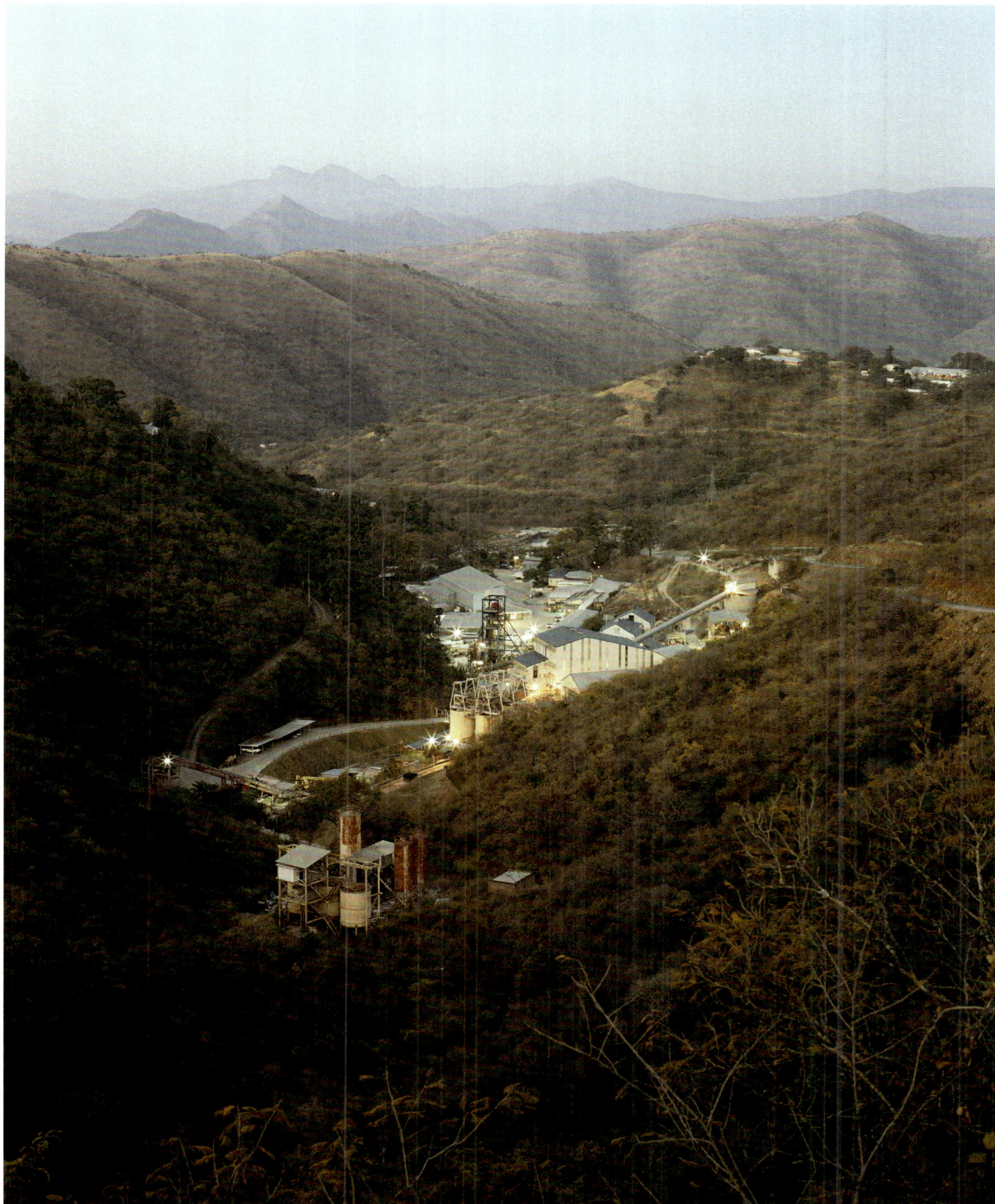

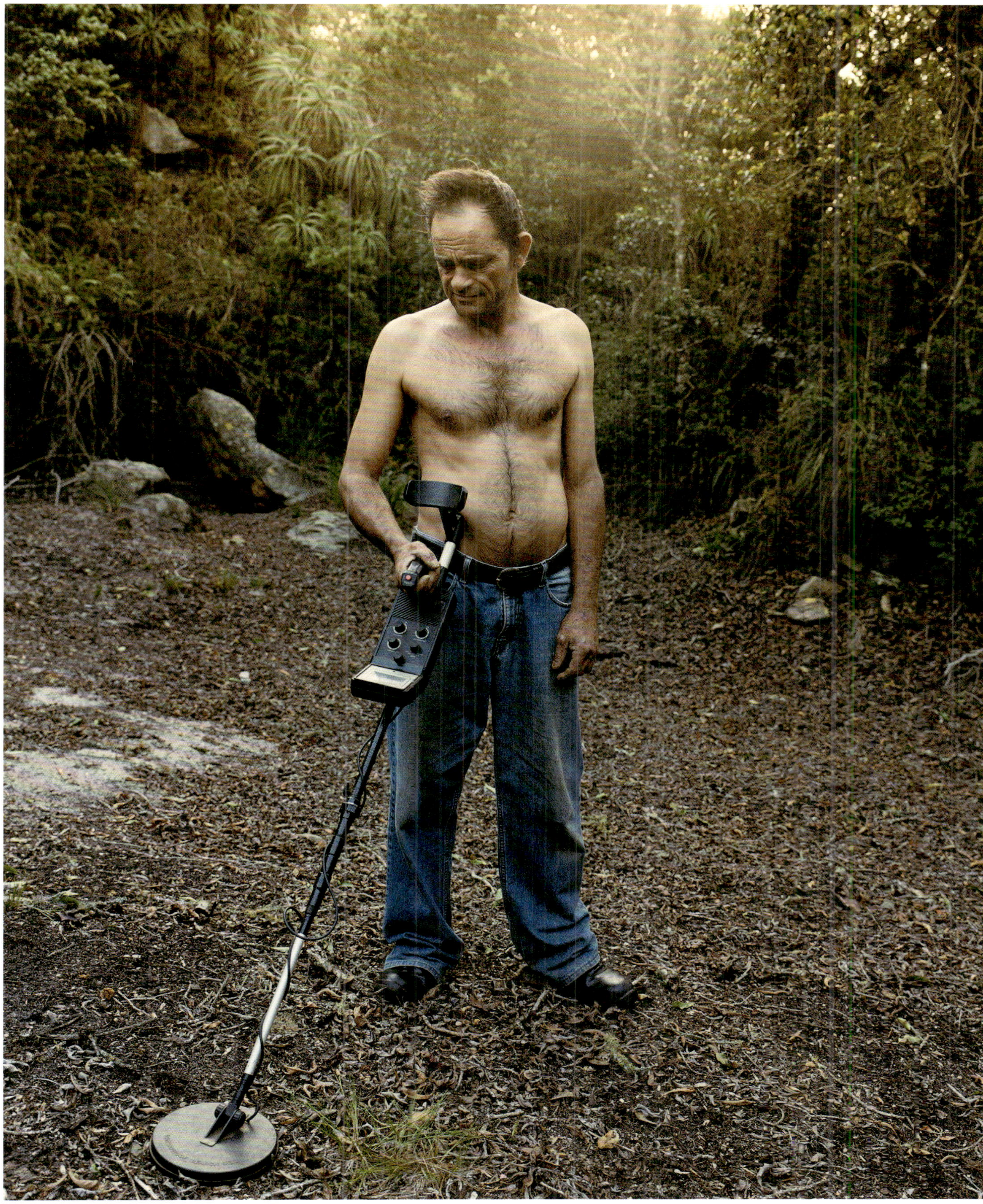

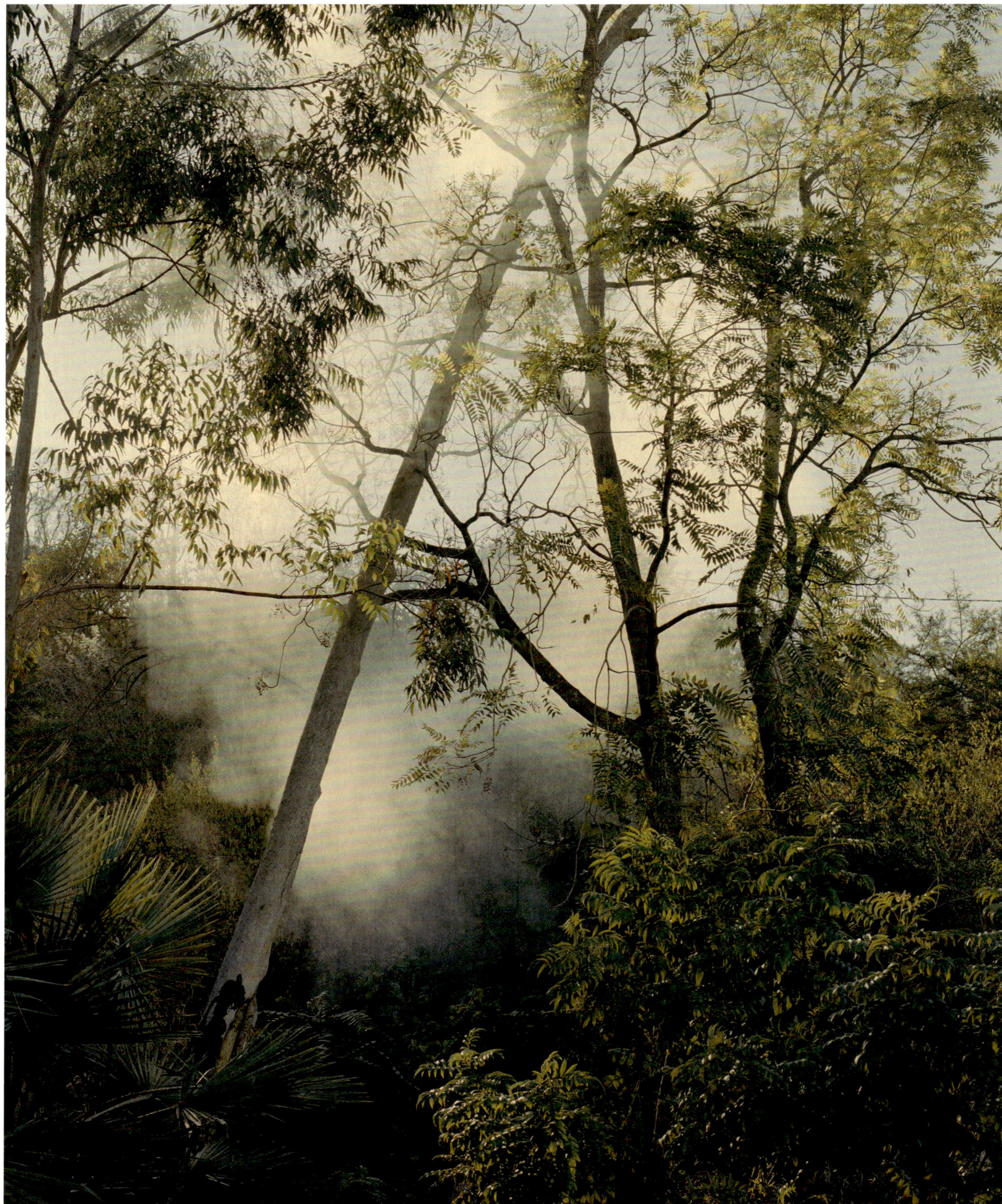

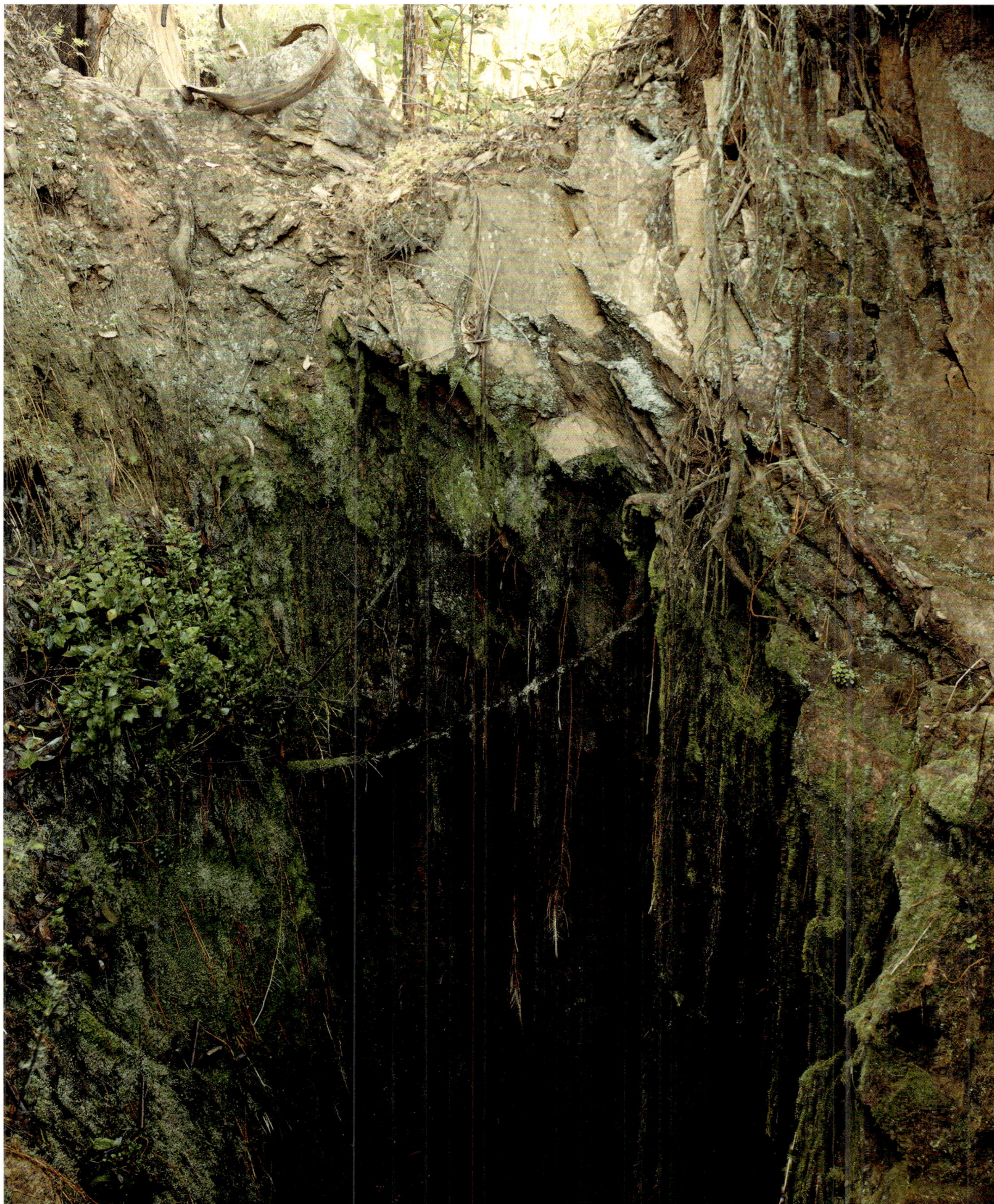

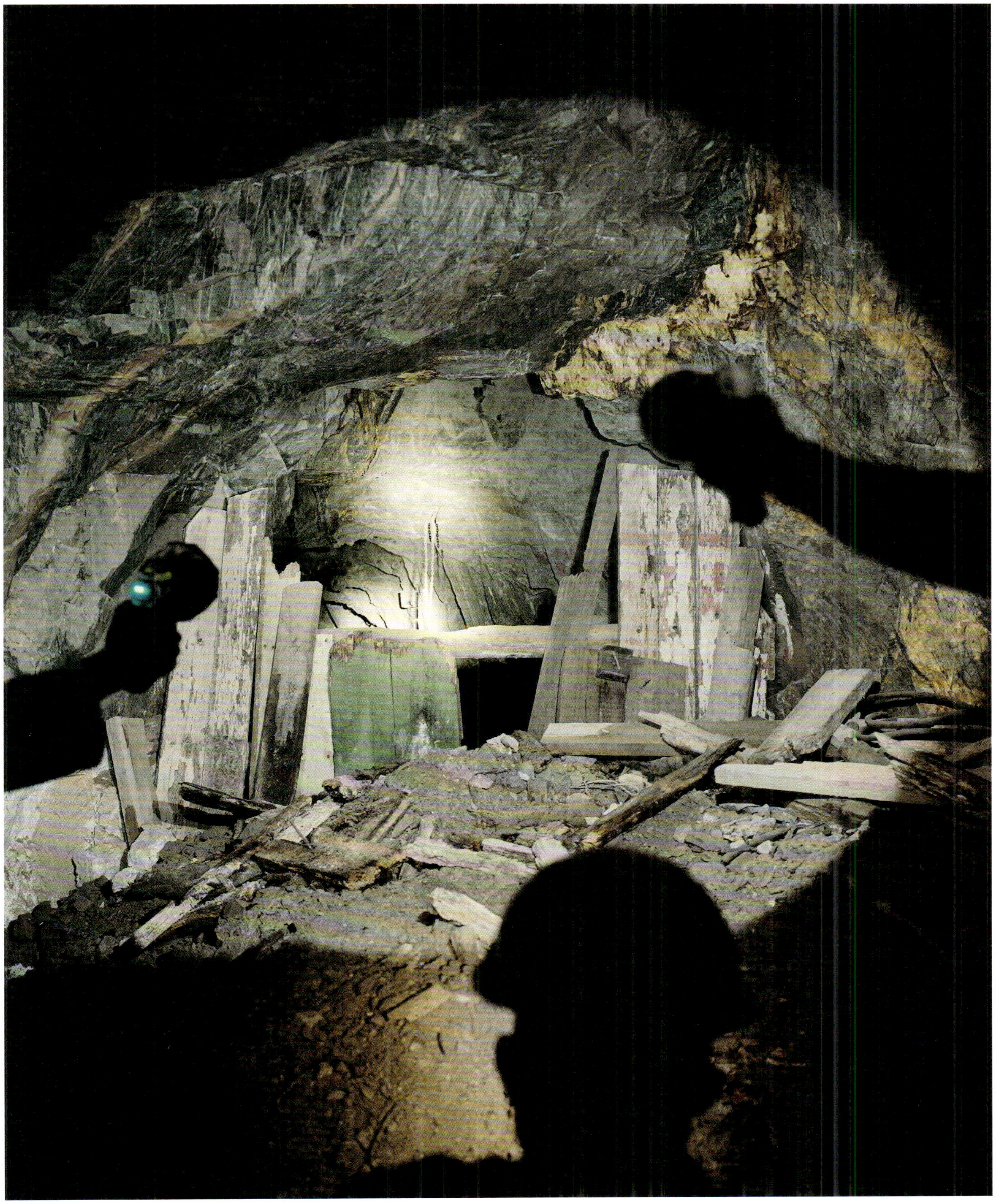

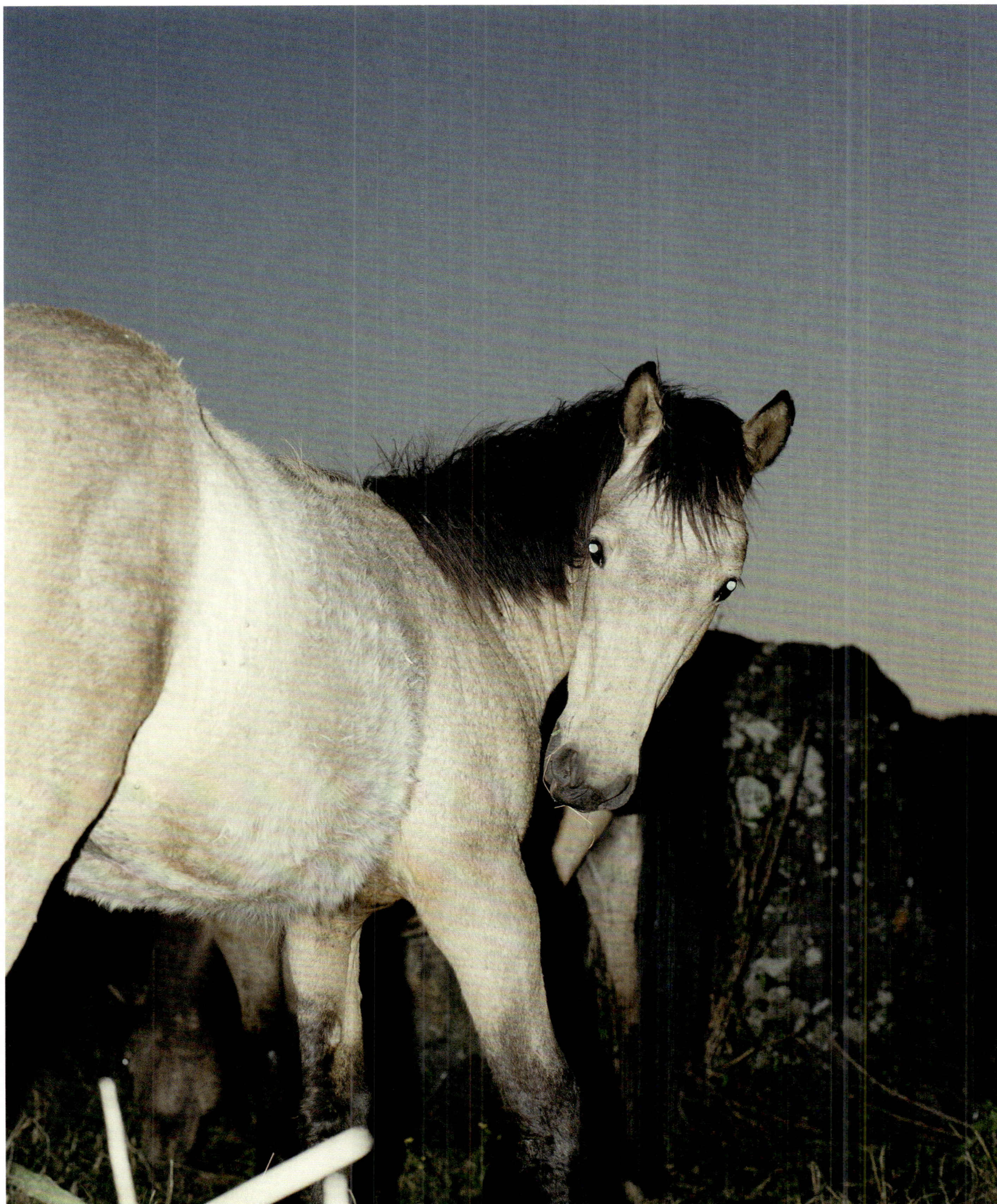

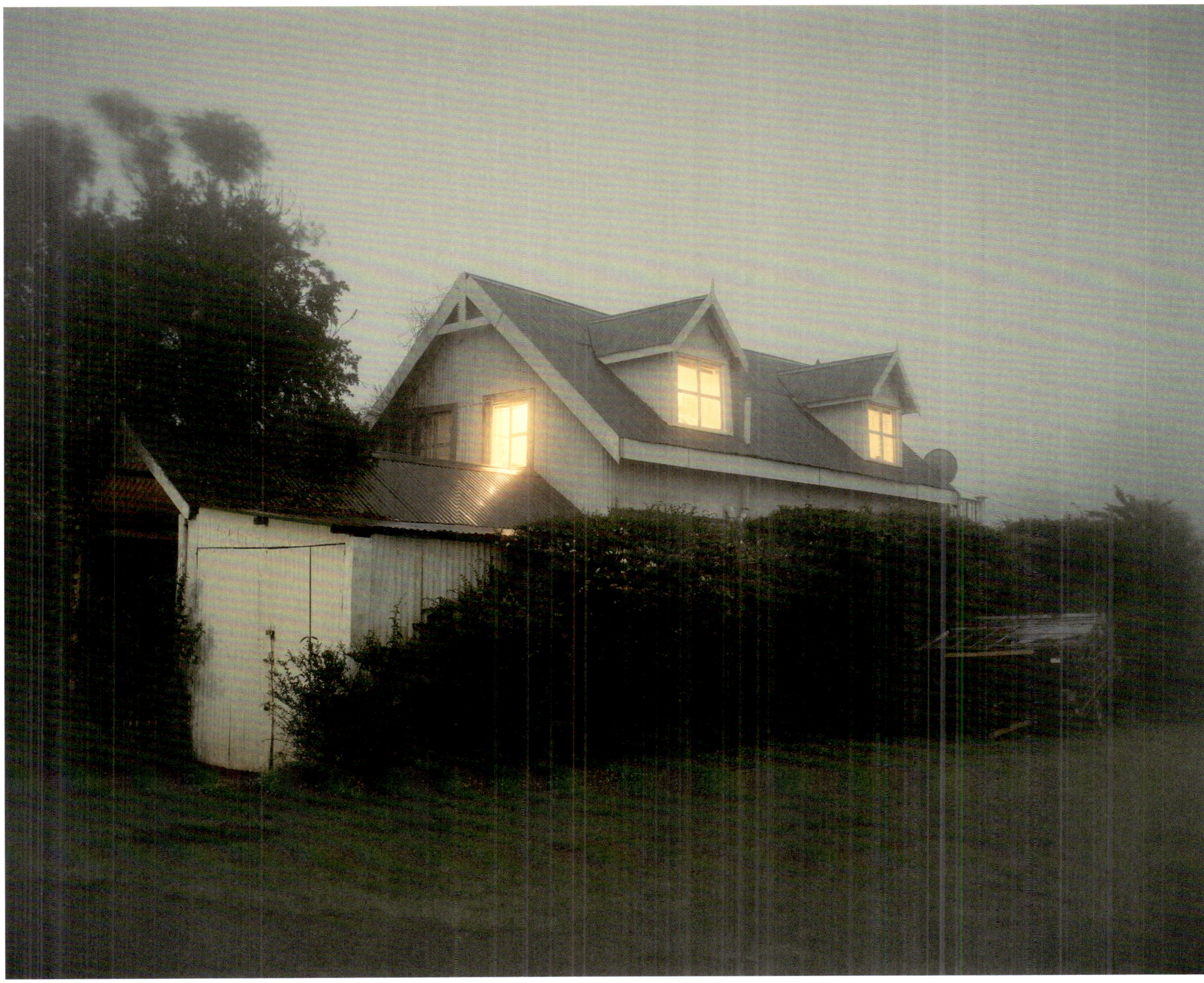

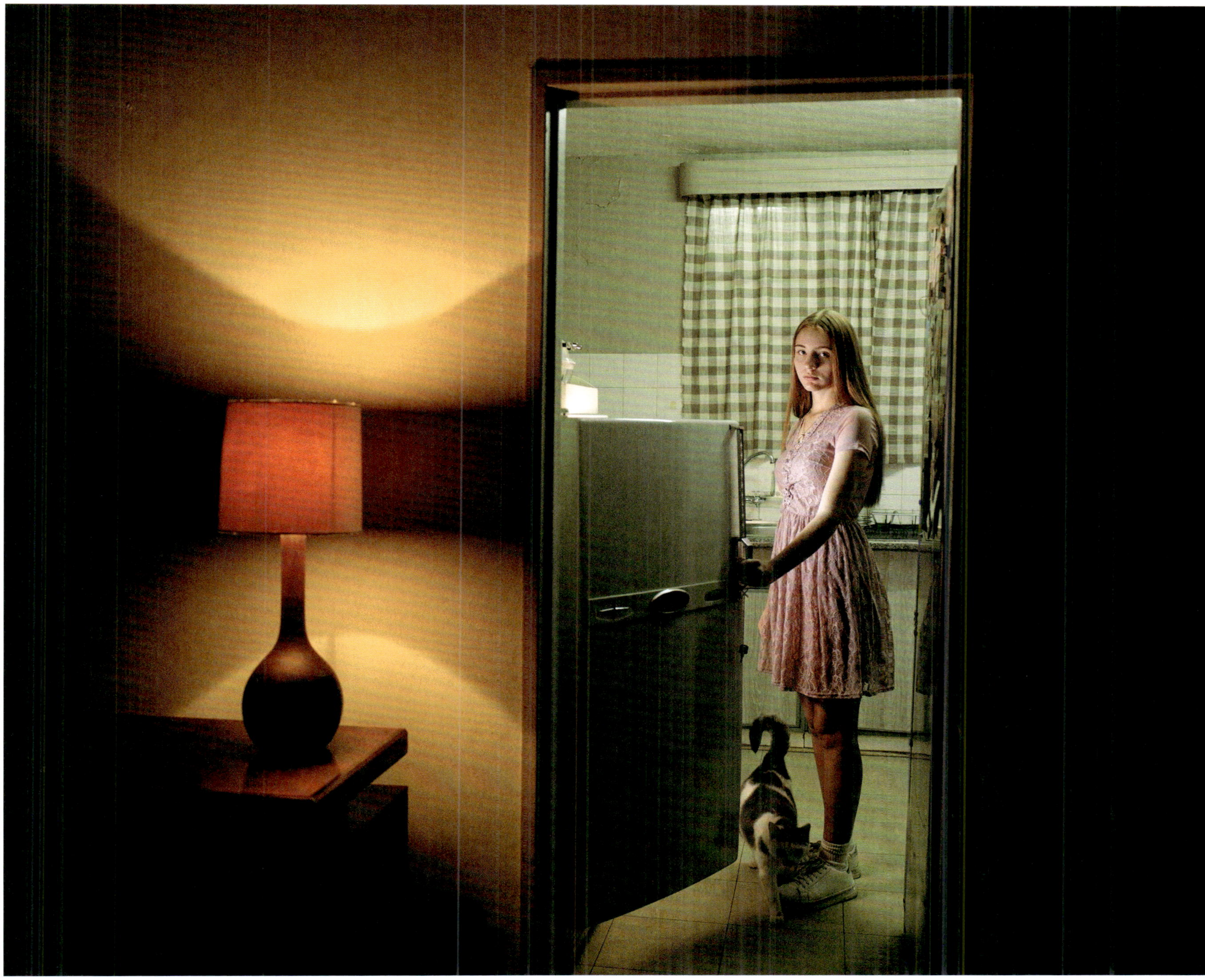

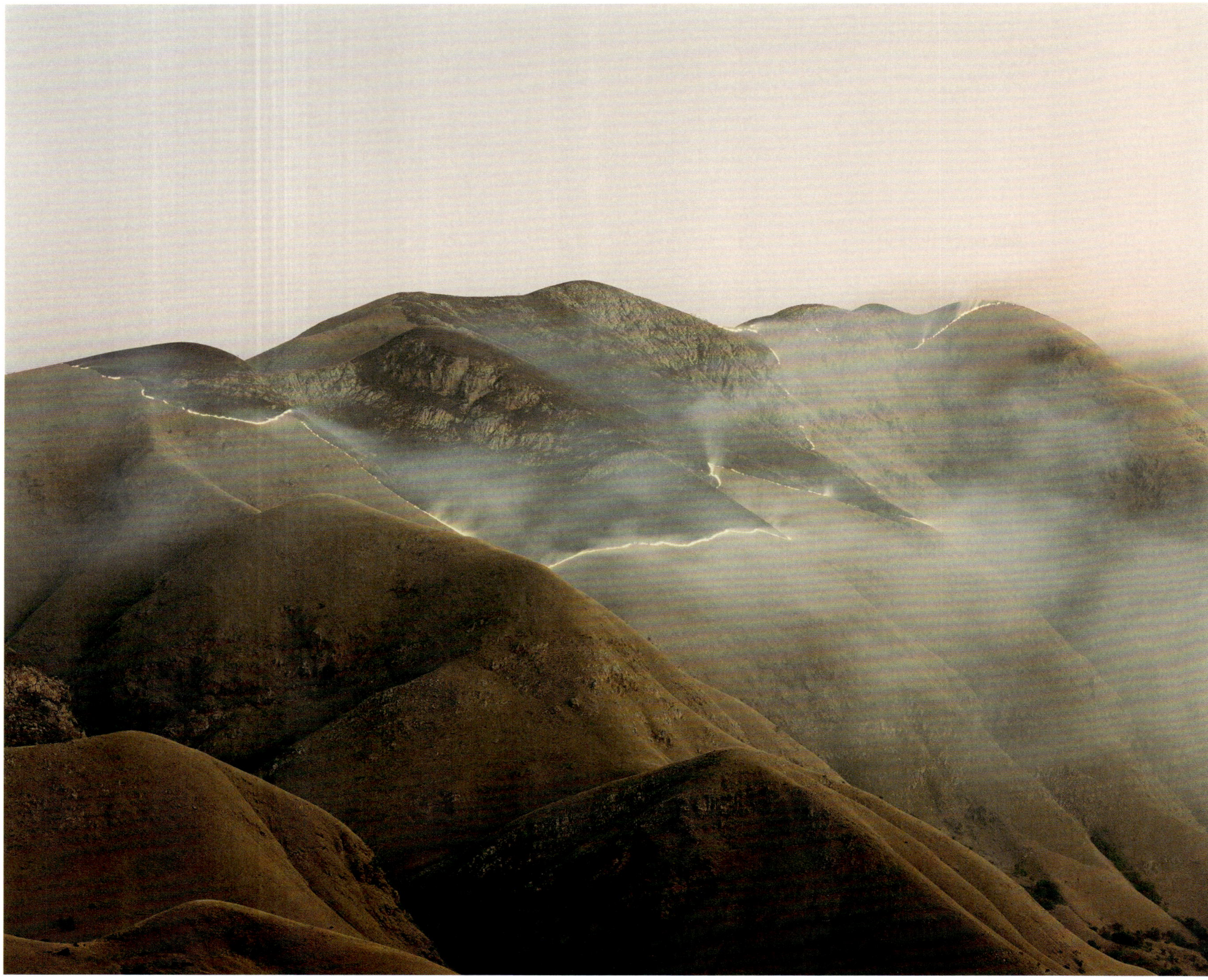

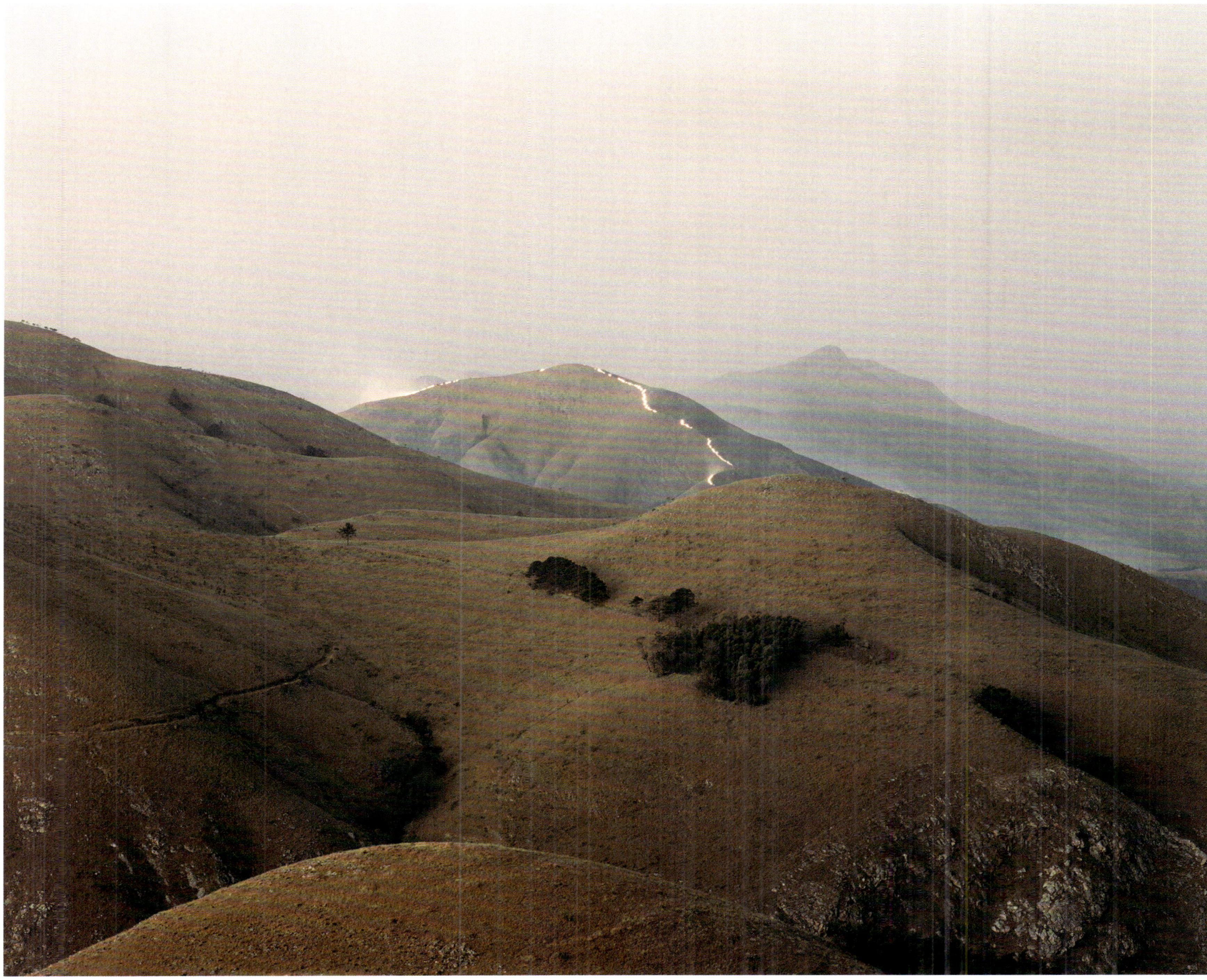

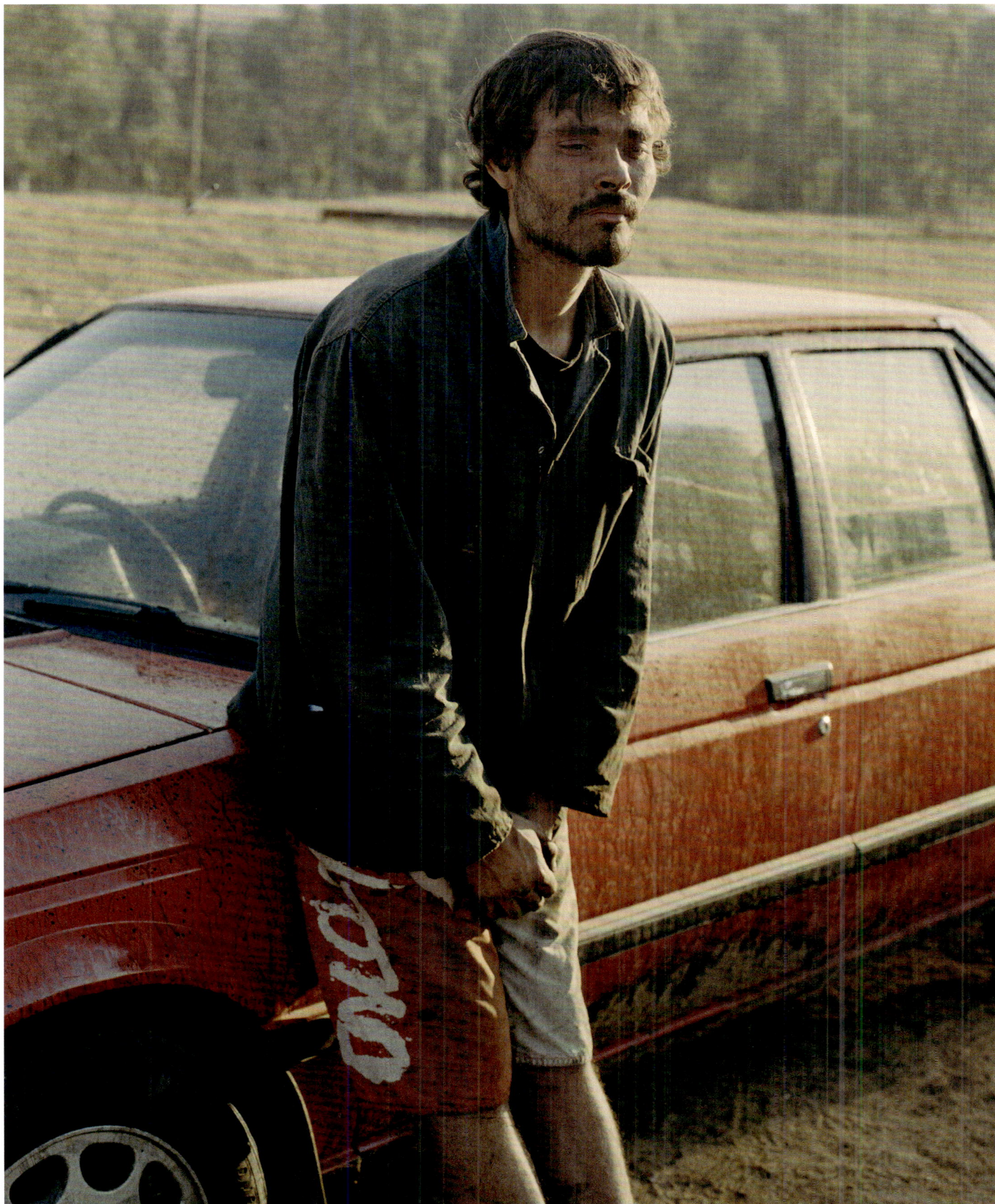

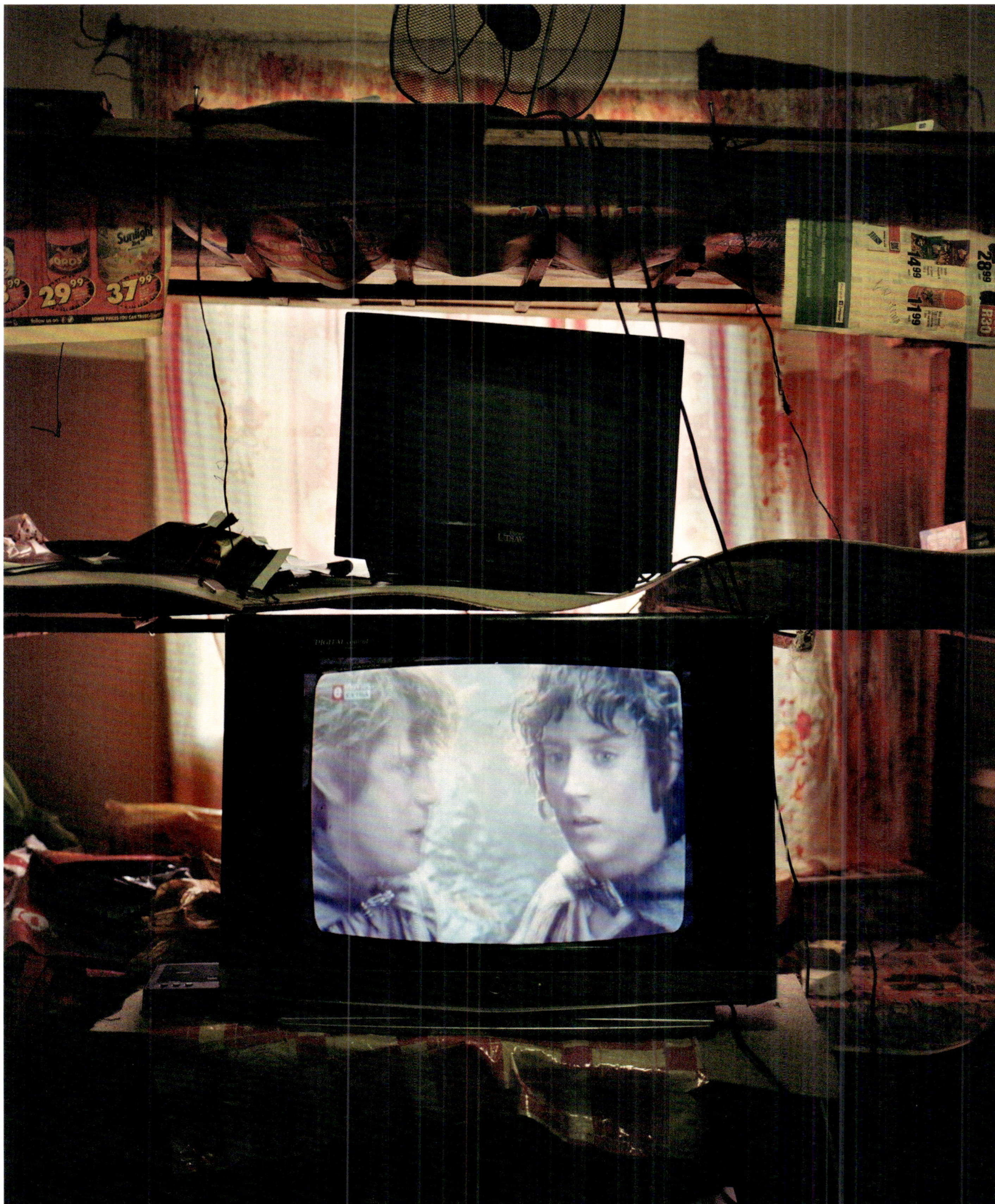
Sunlight

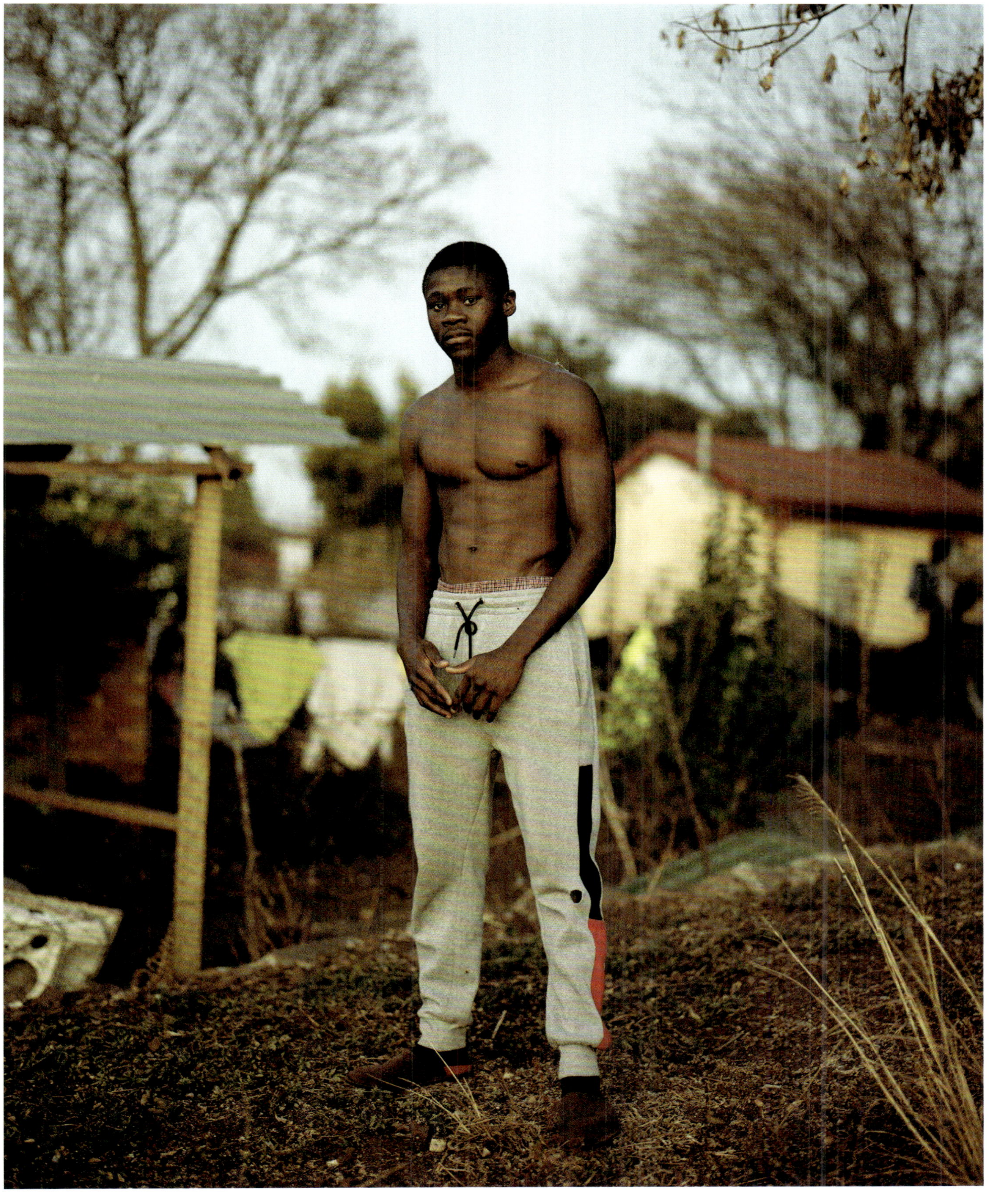

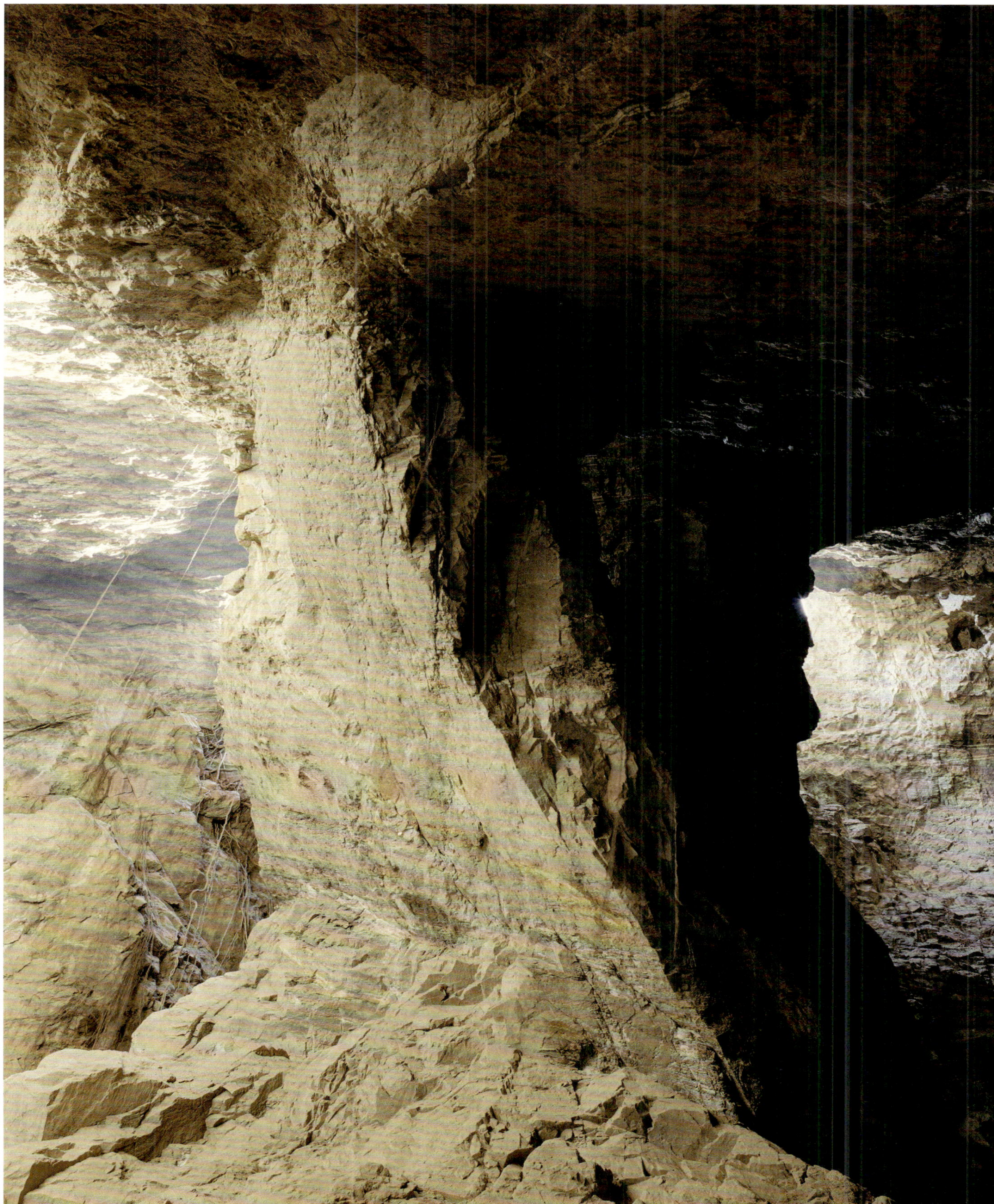

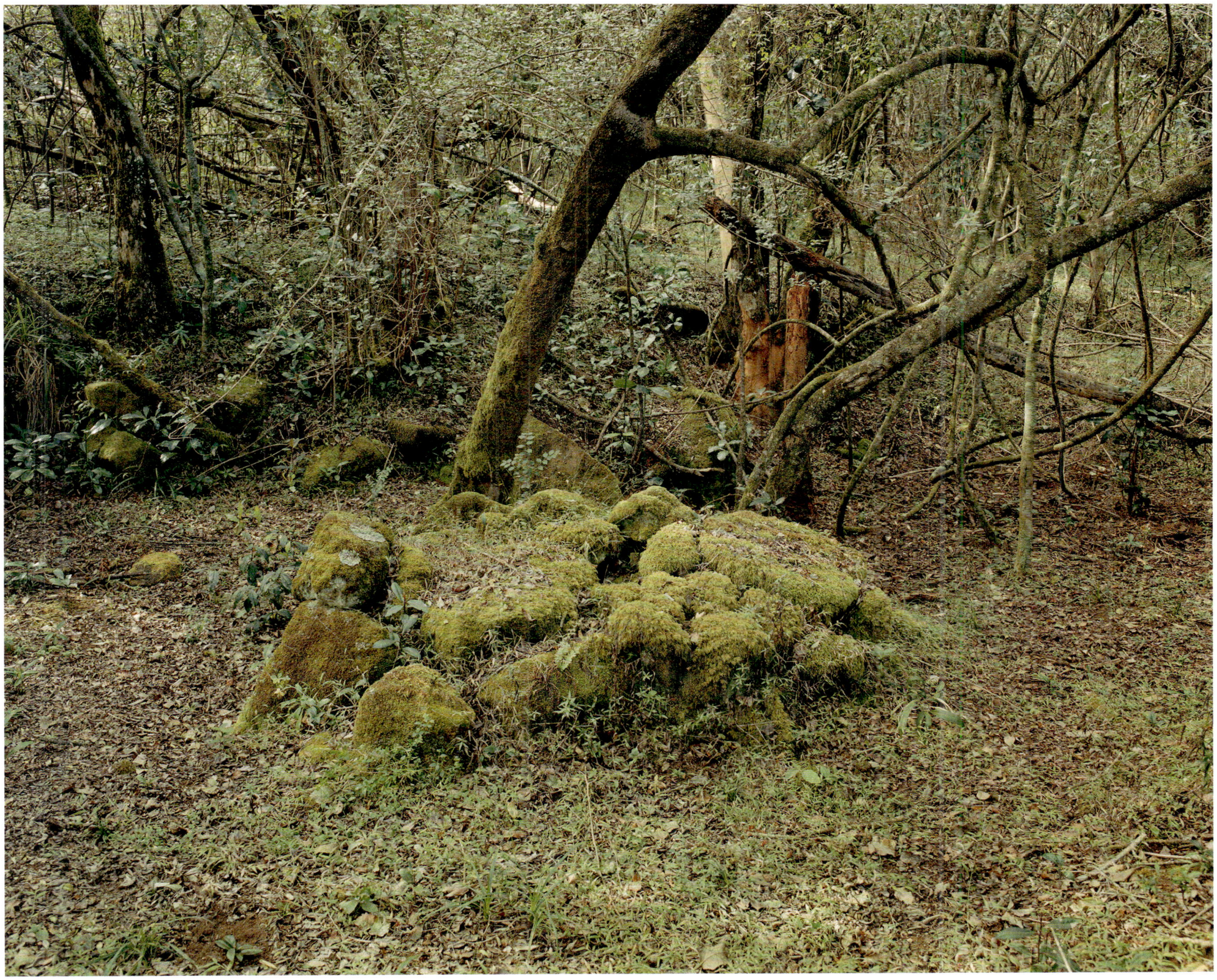

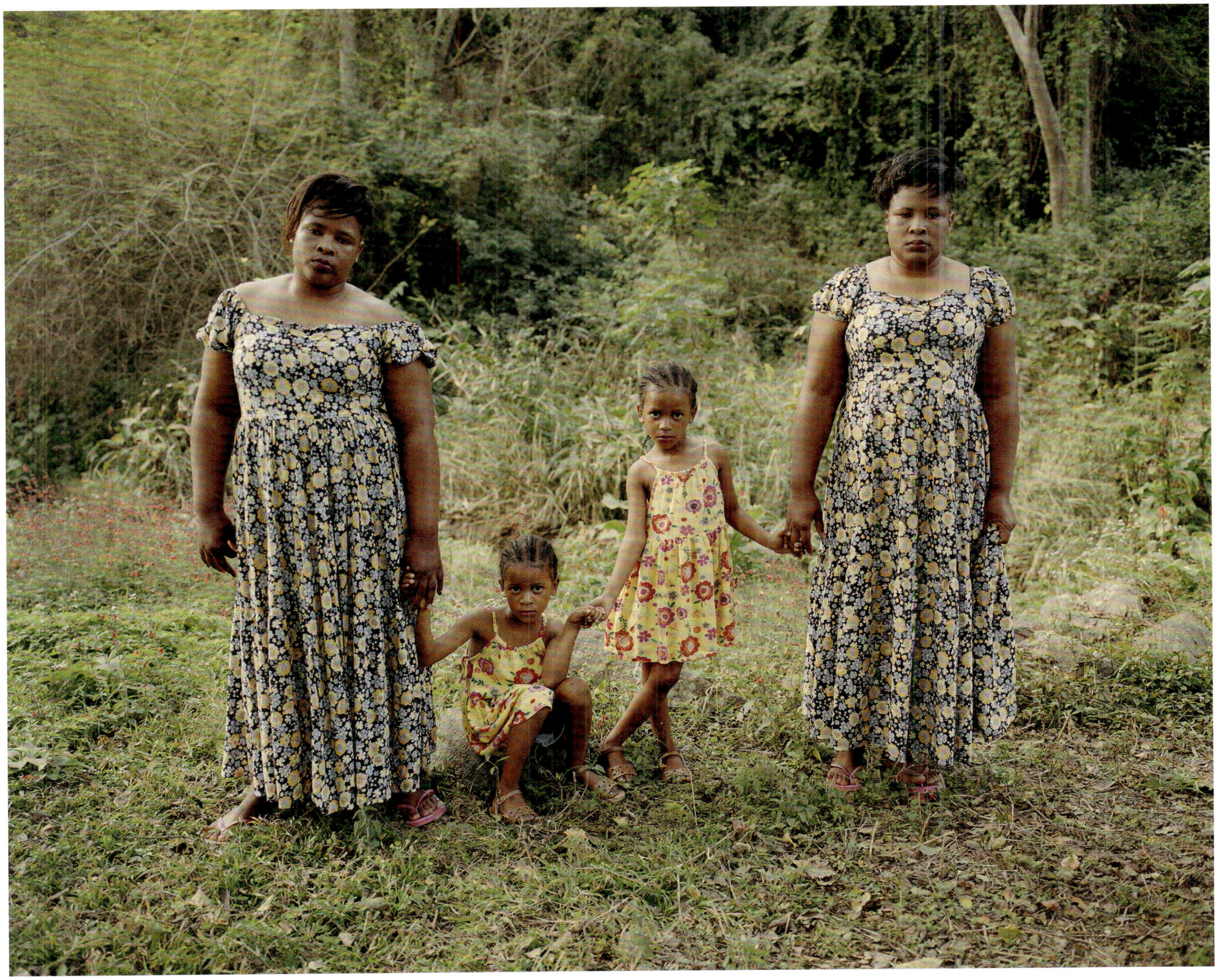

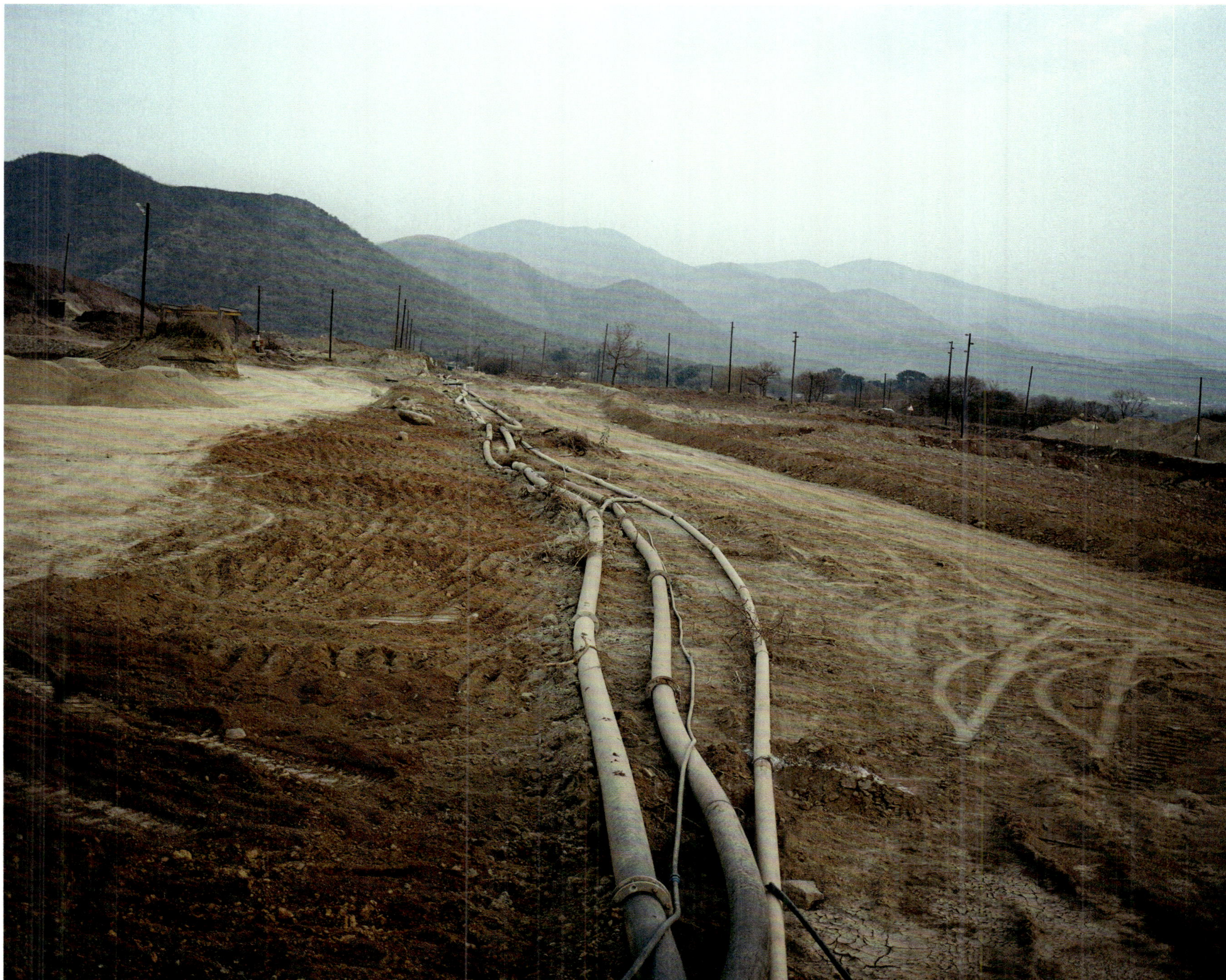

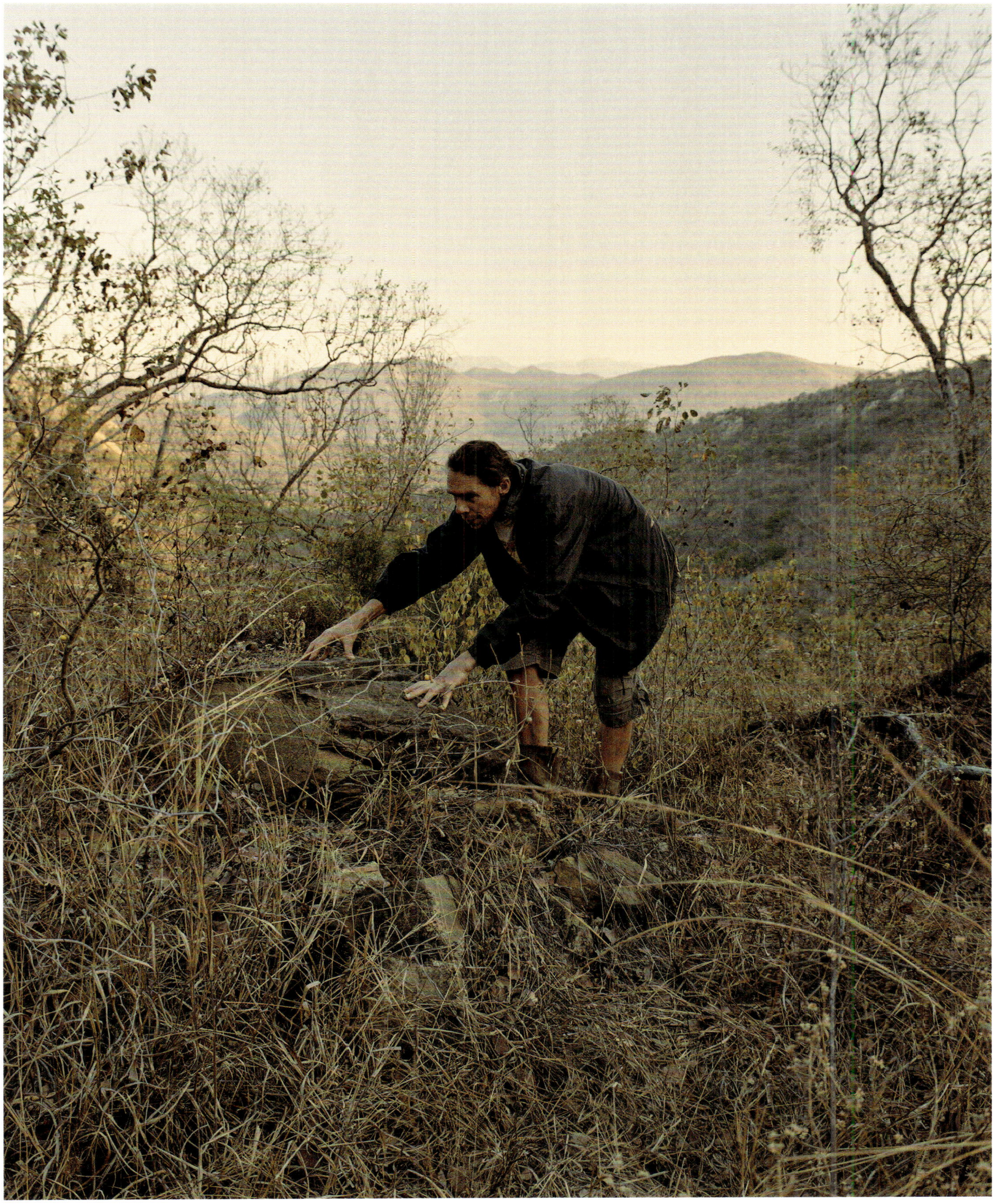

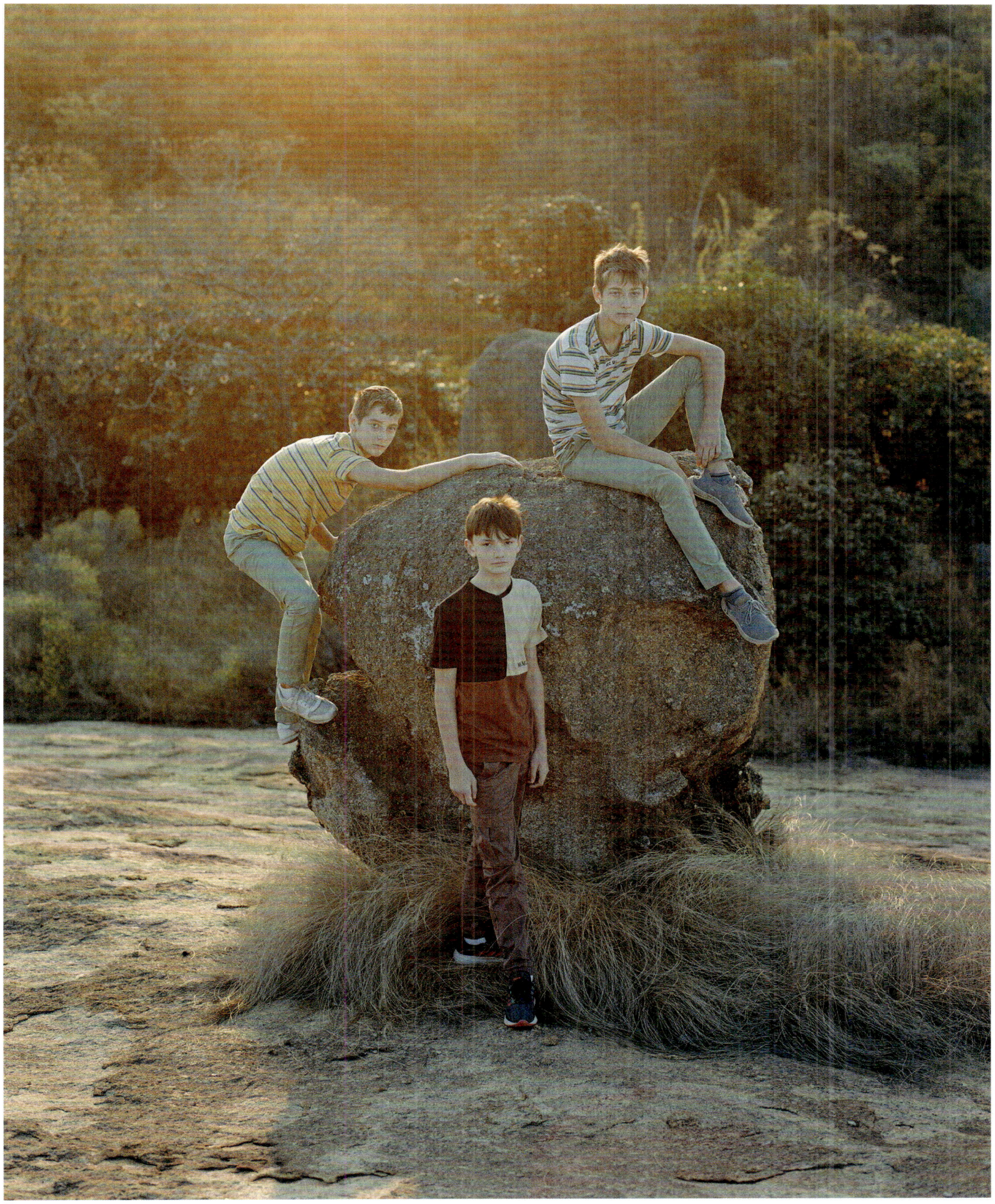

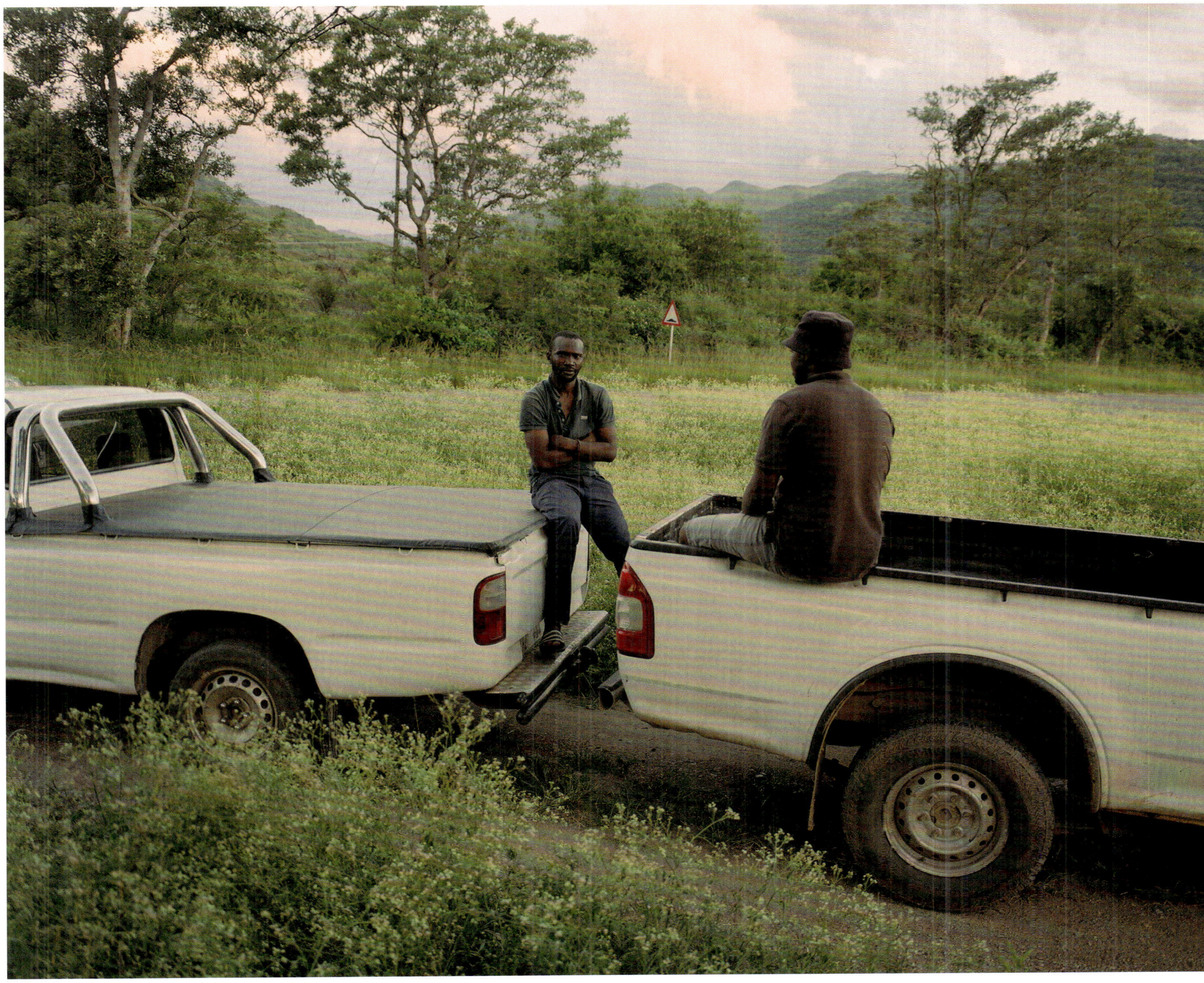

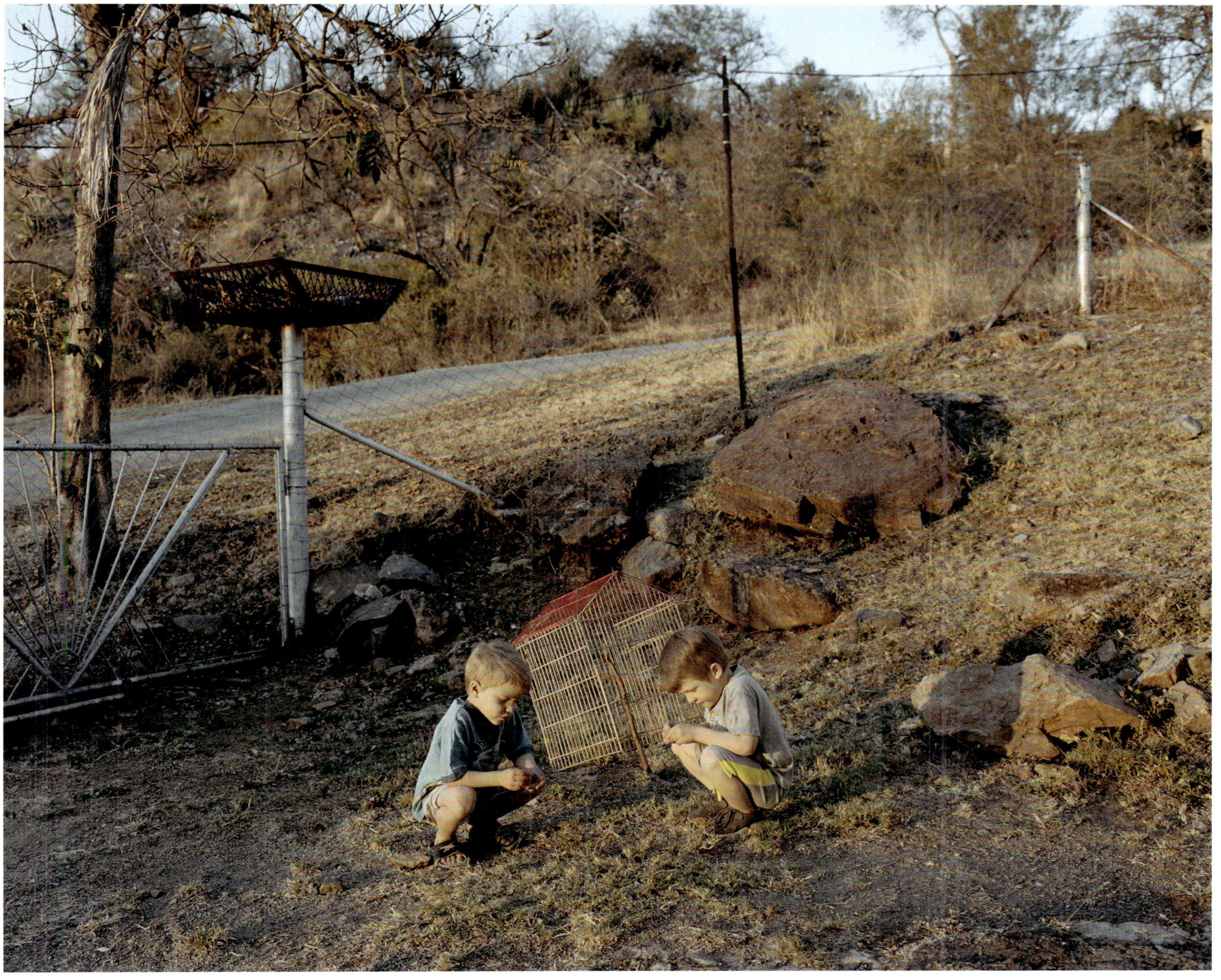

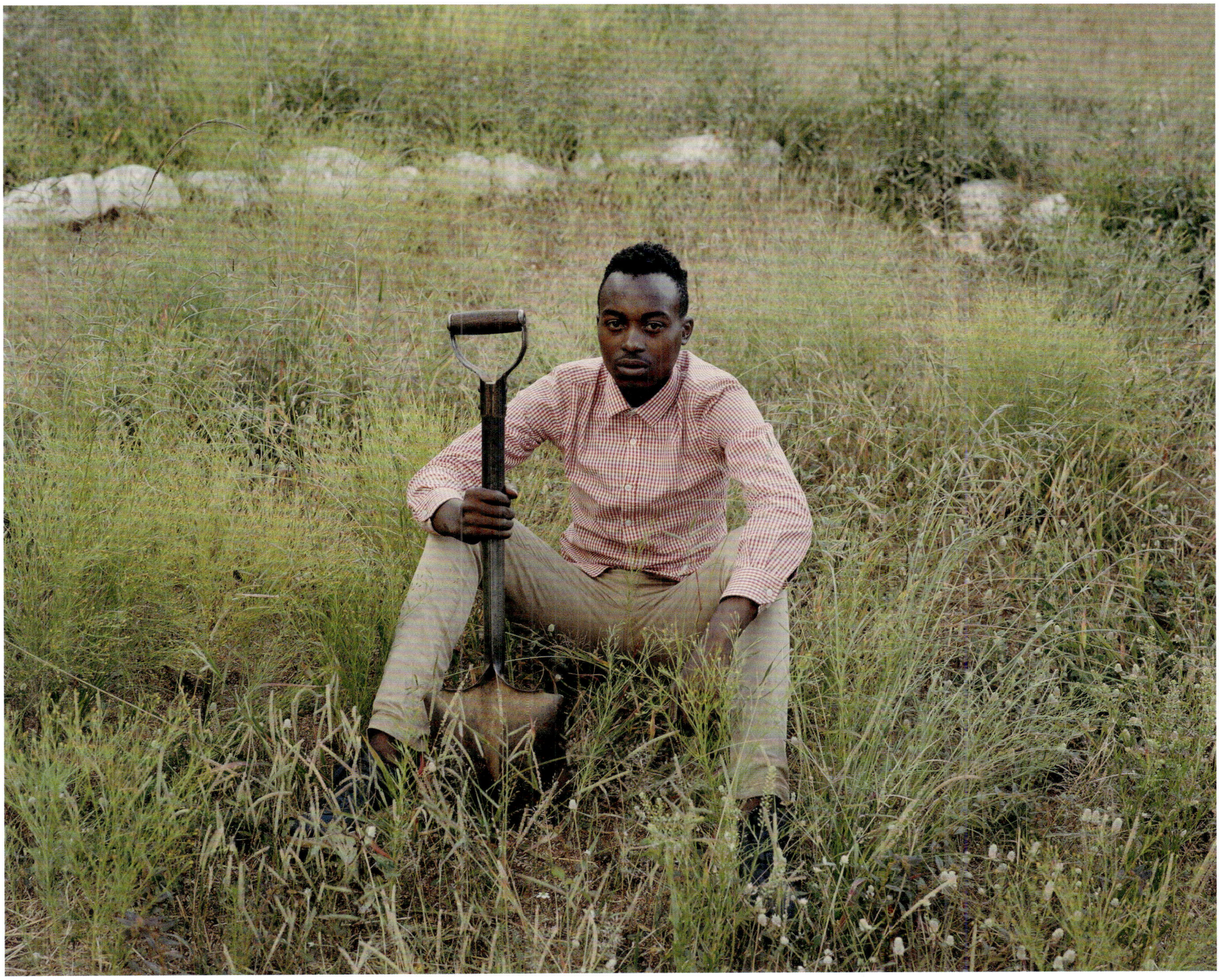

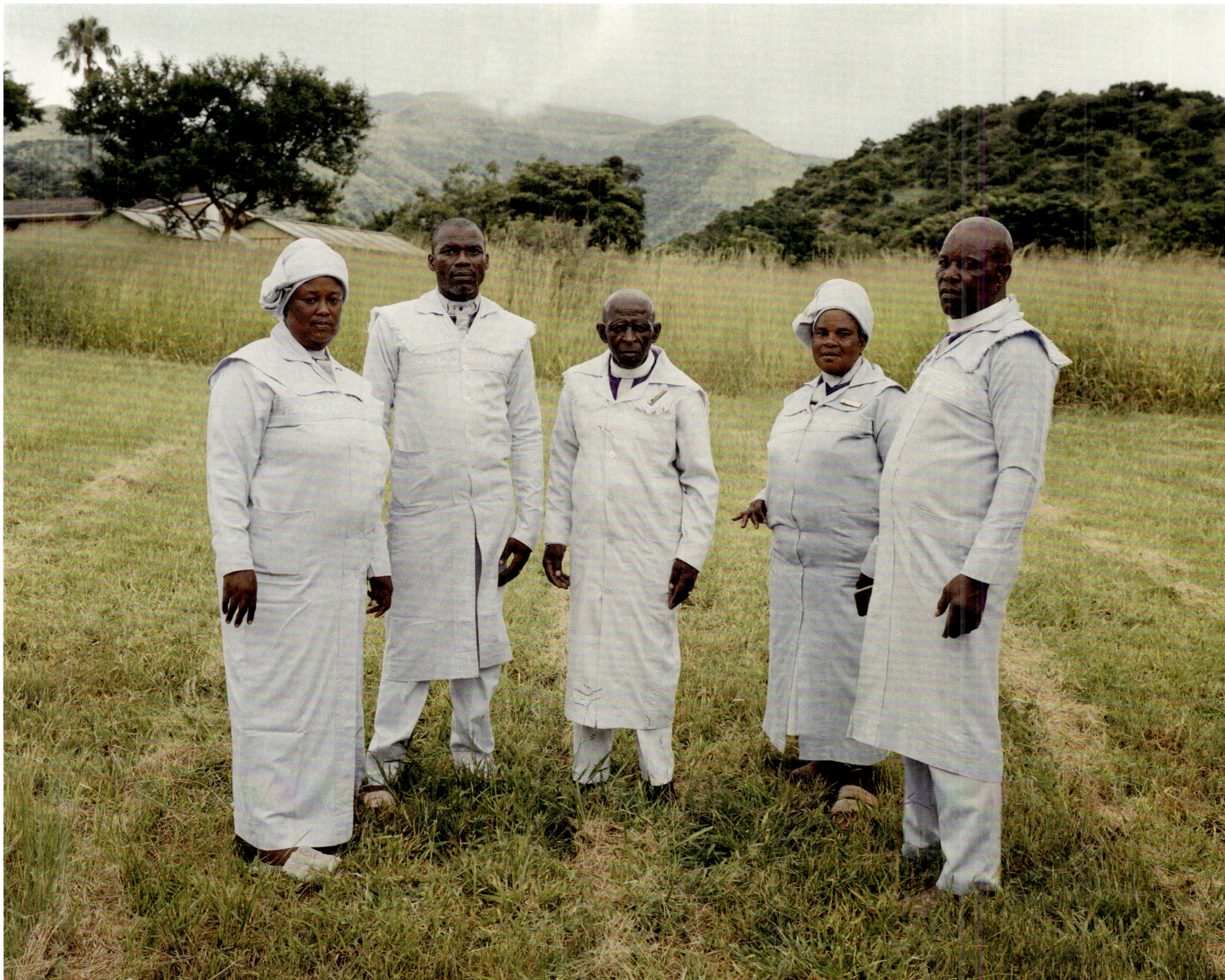

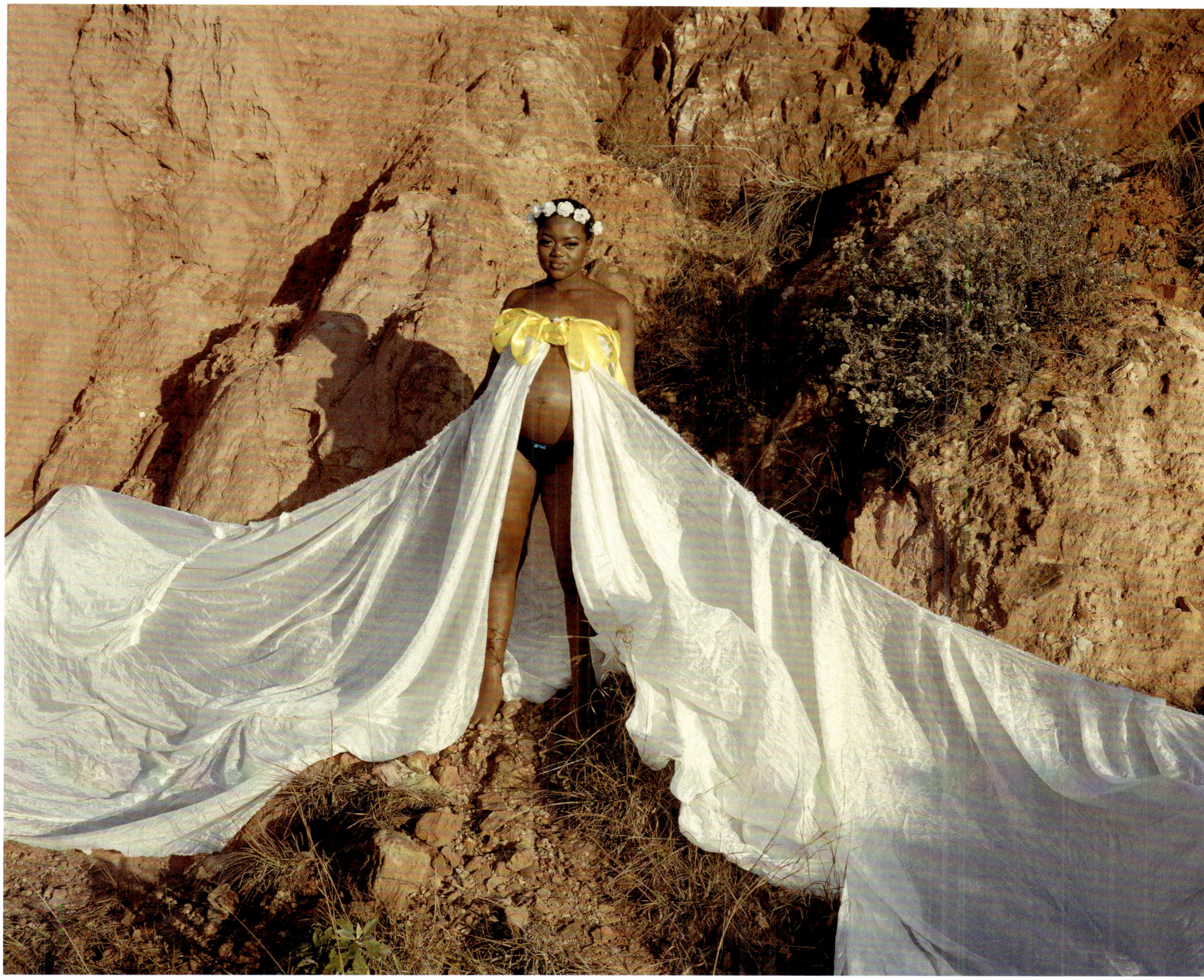

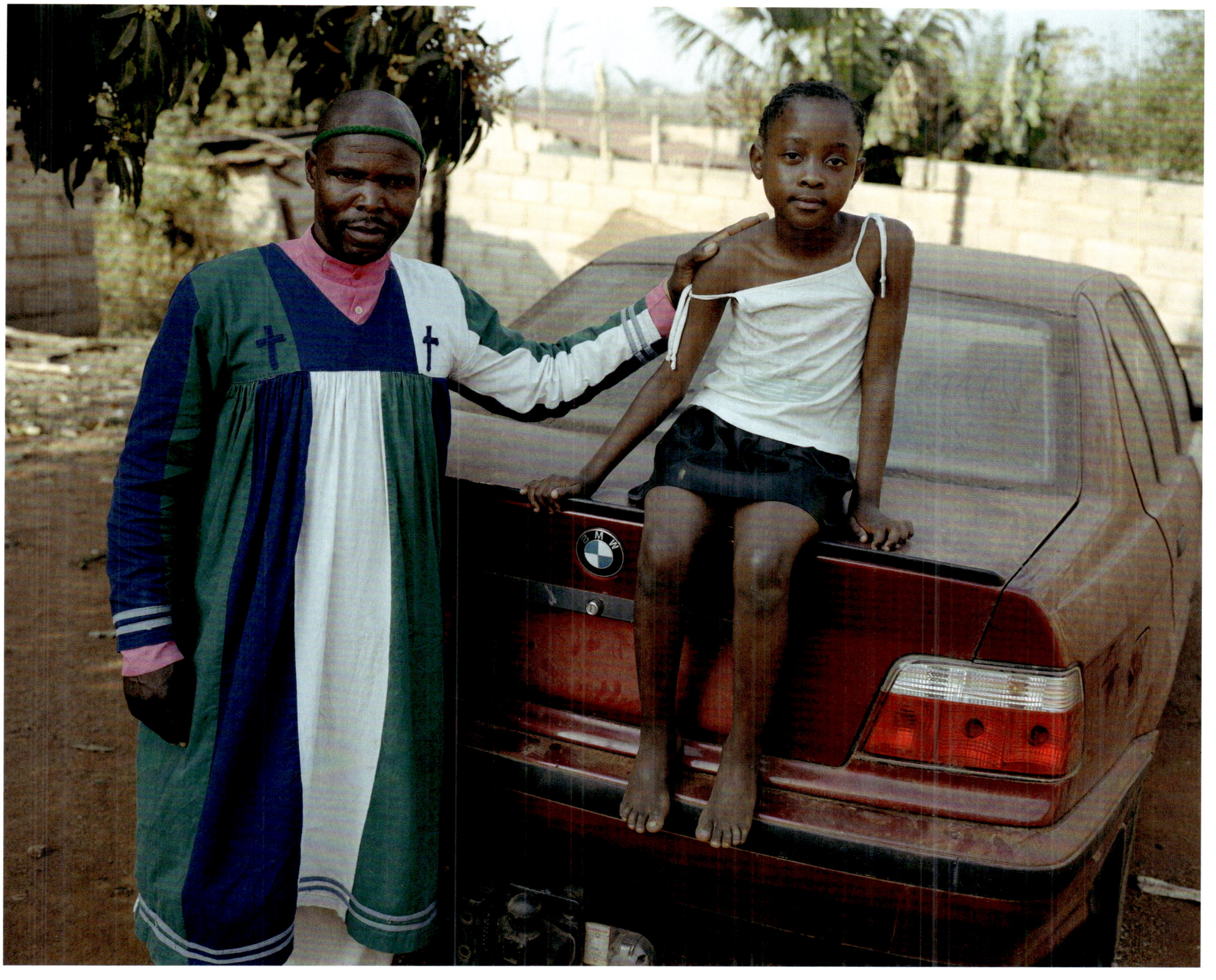
BMW

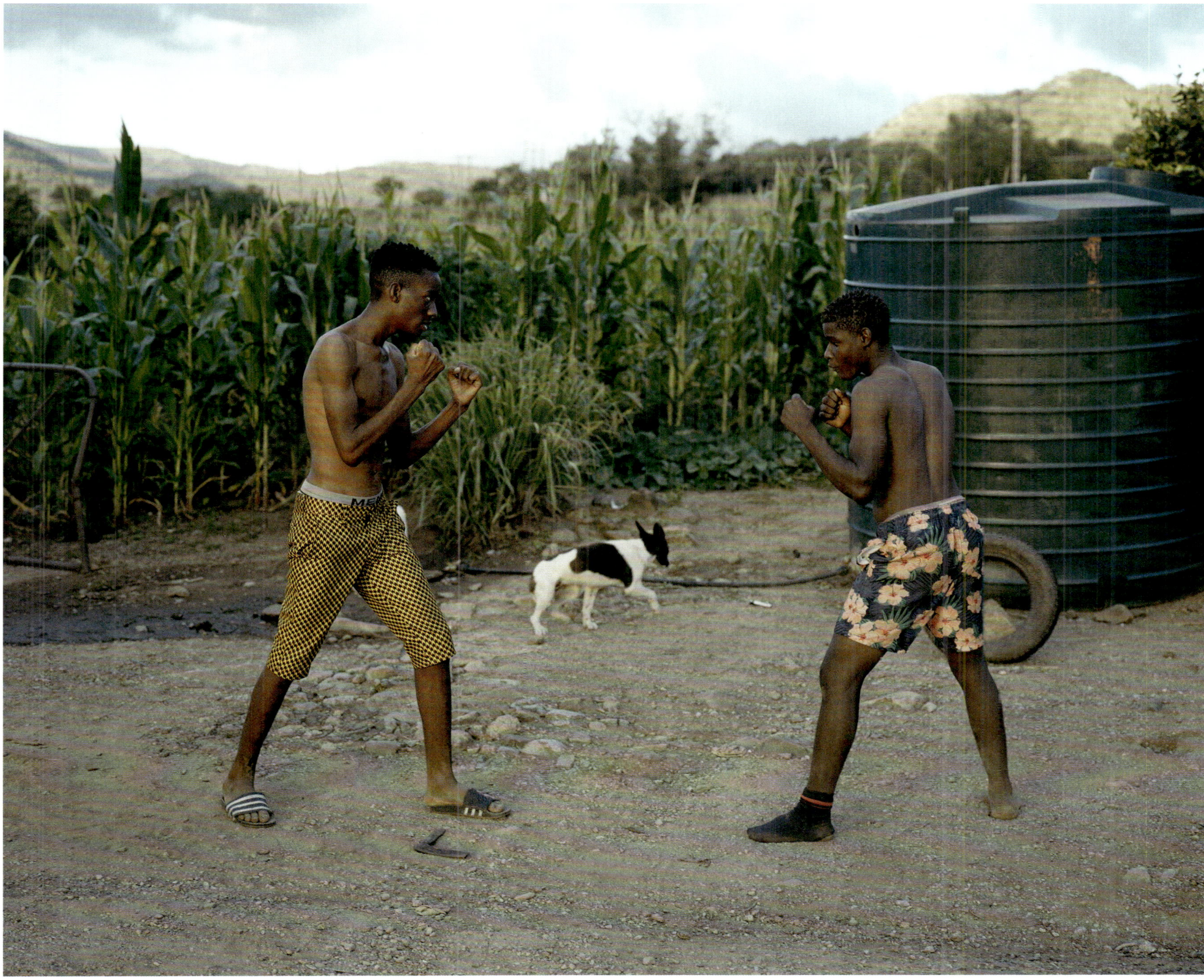

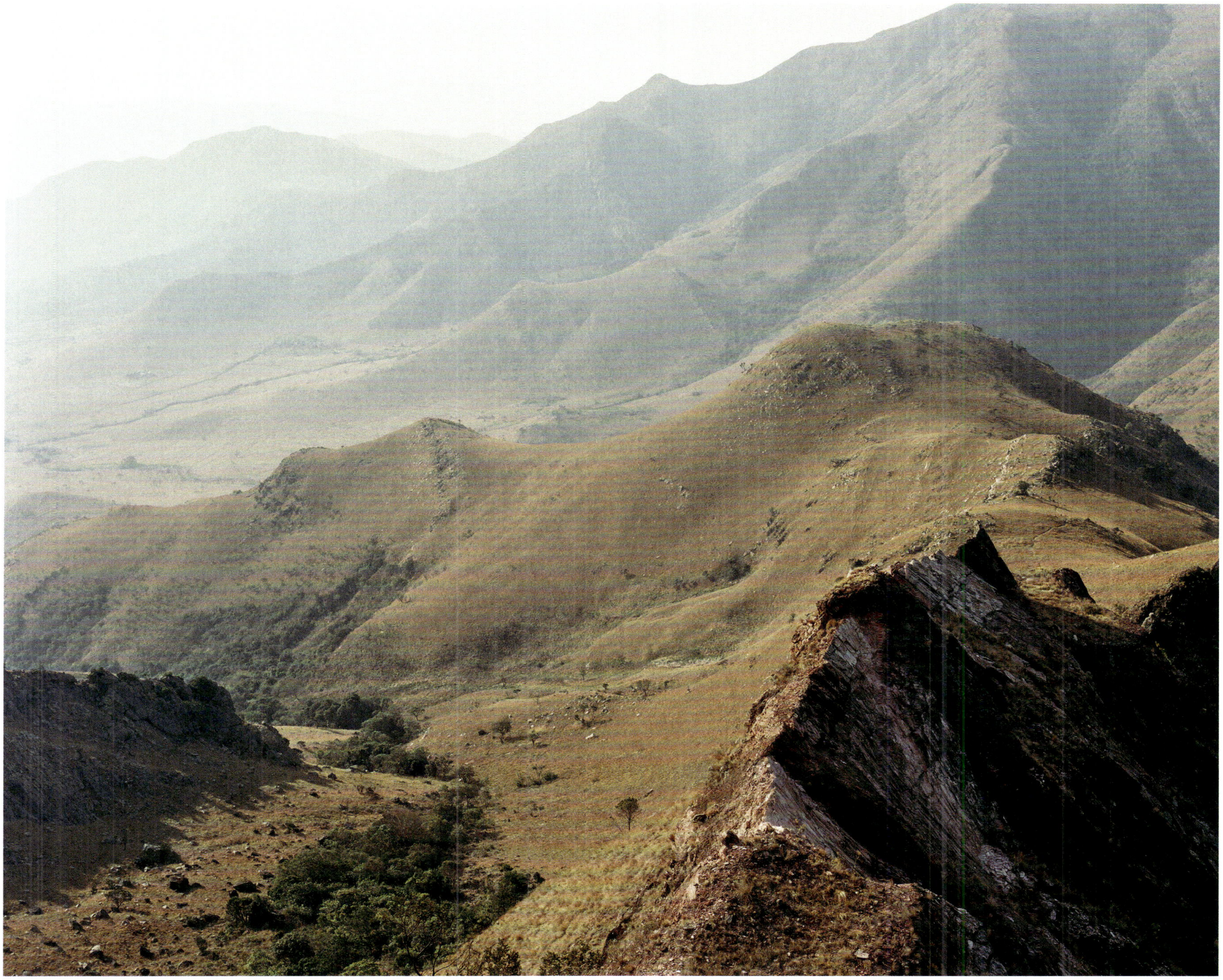

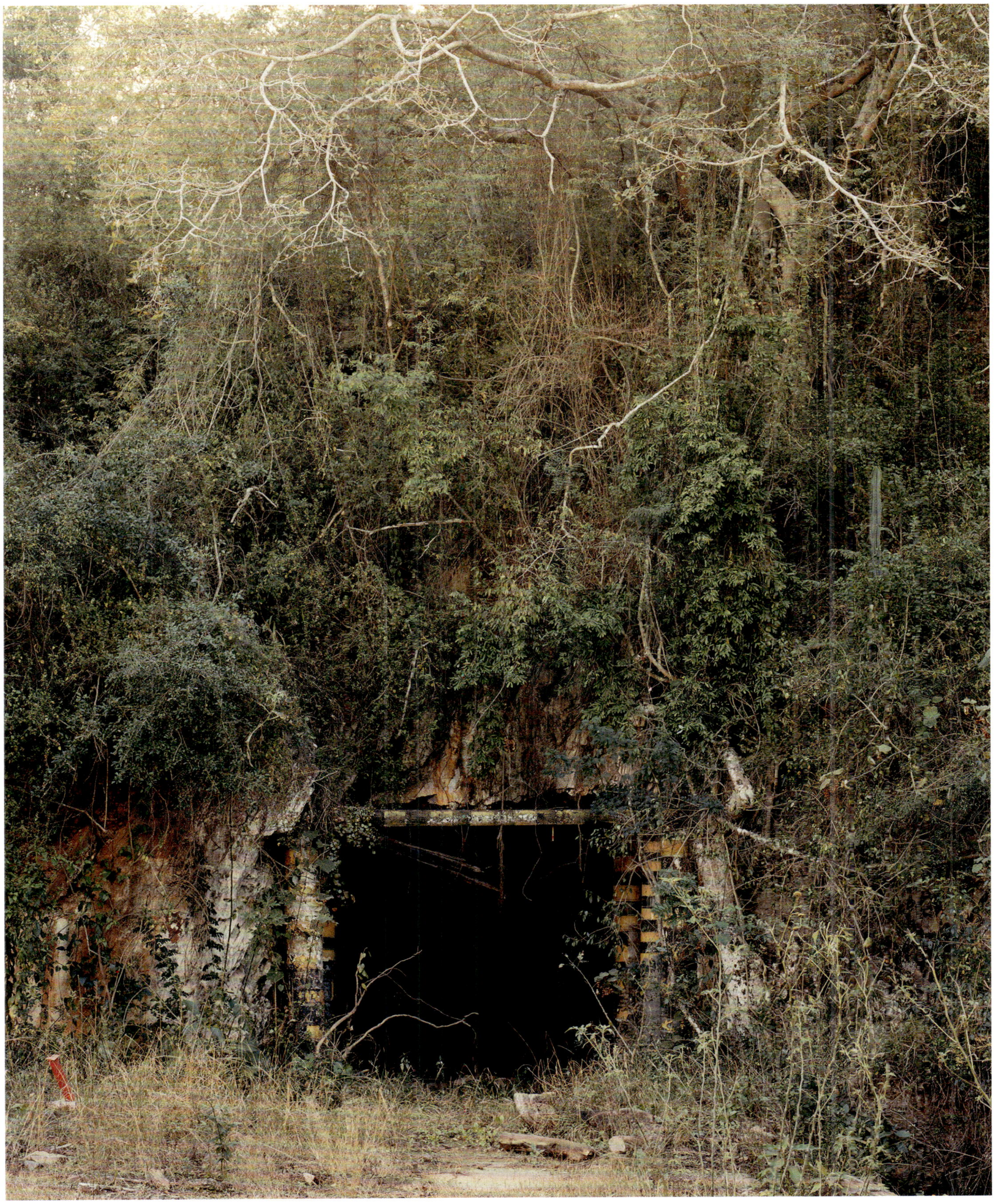

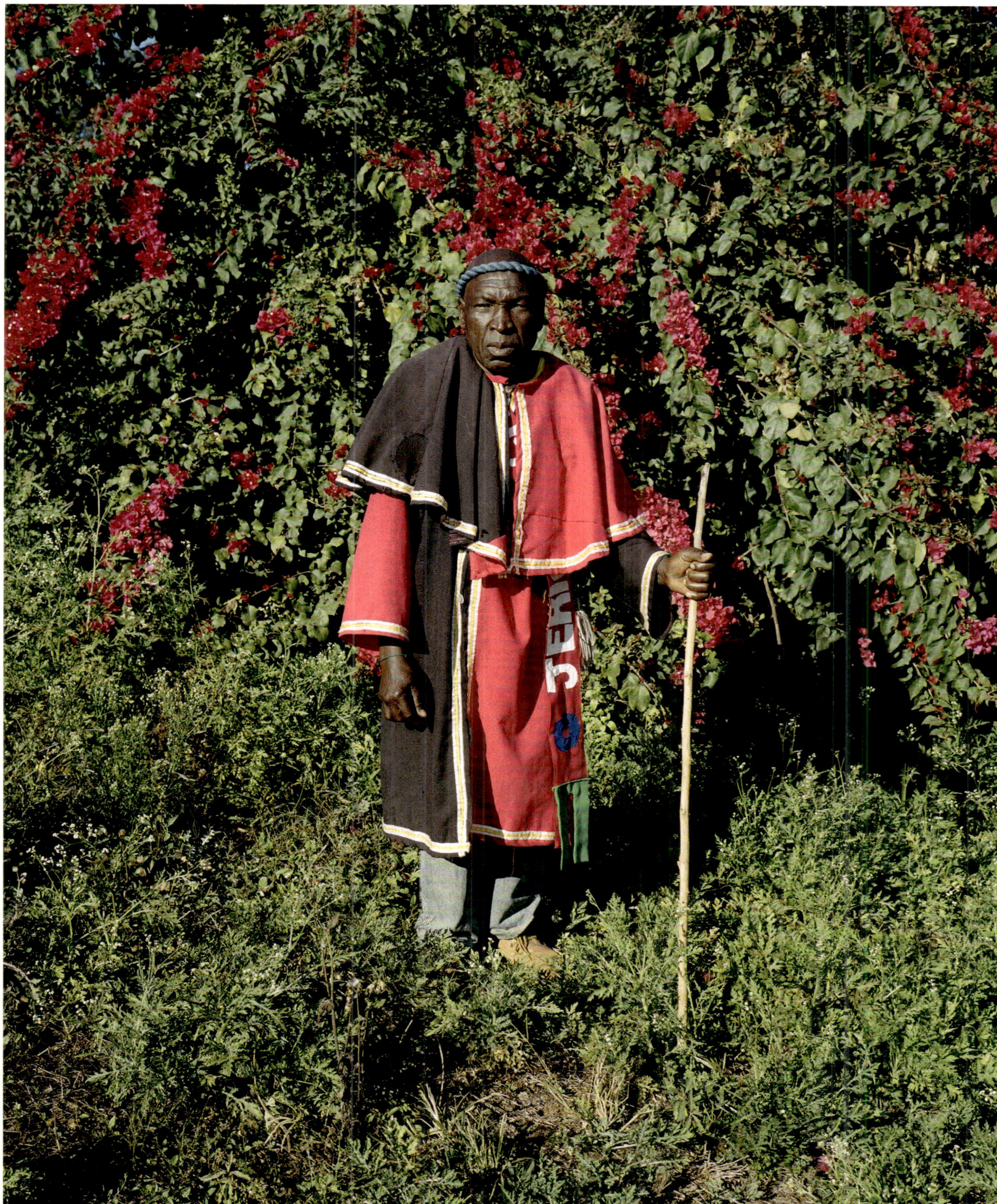

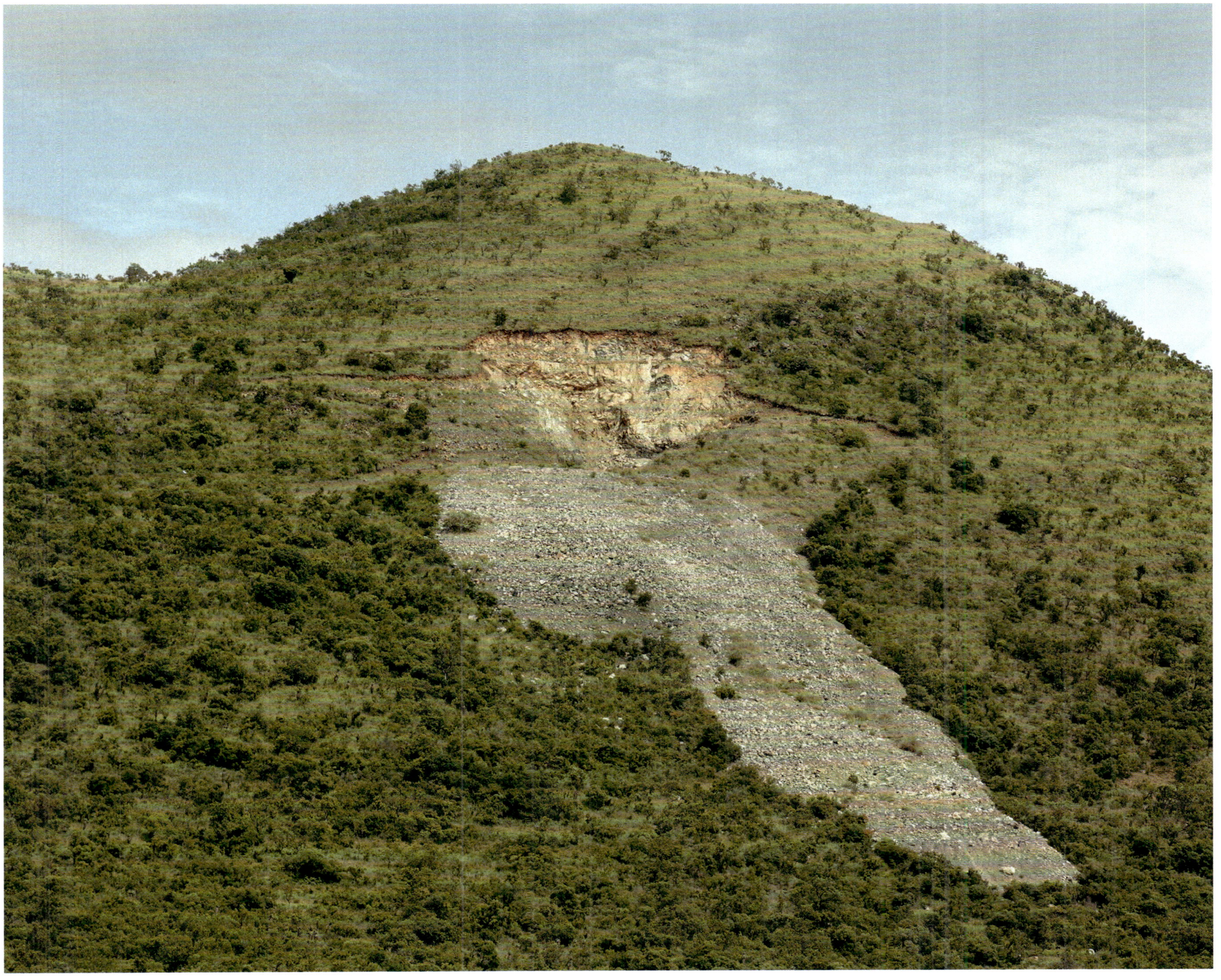

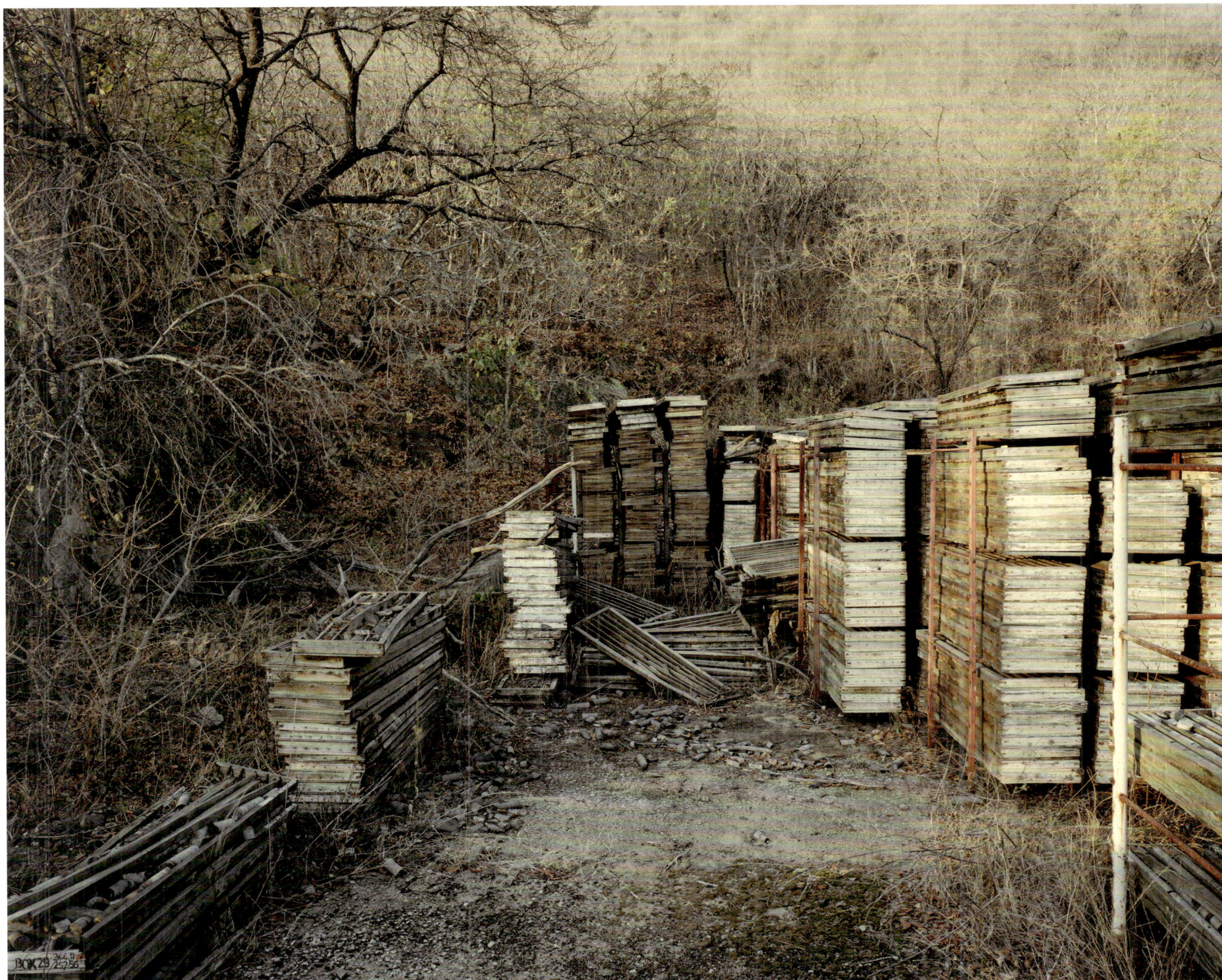
BOX29

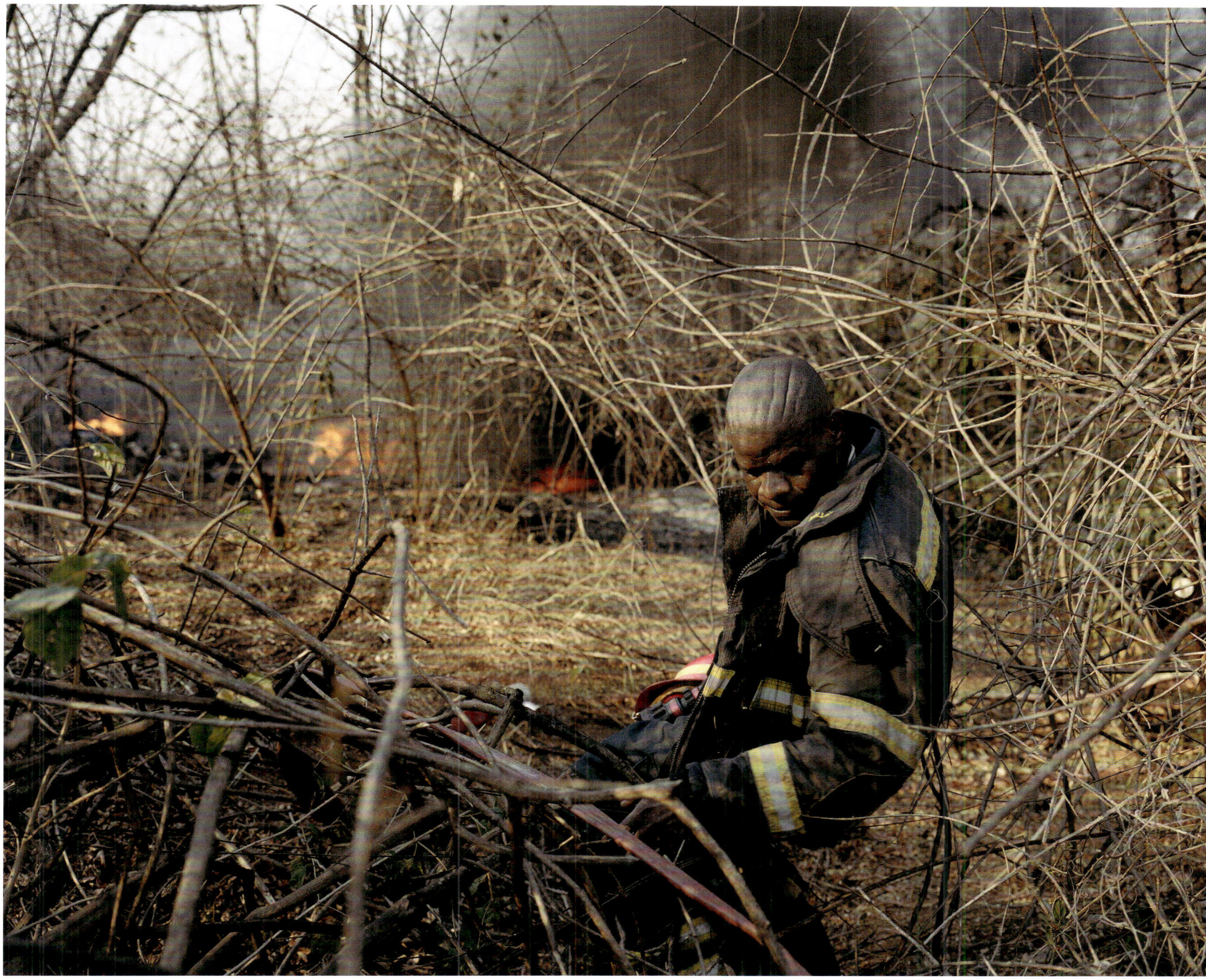

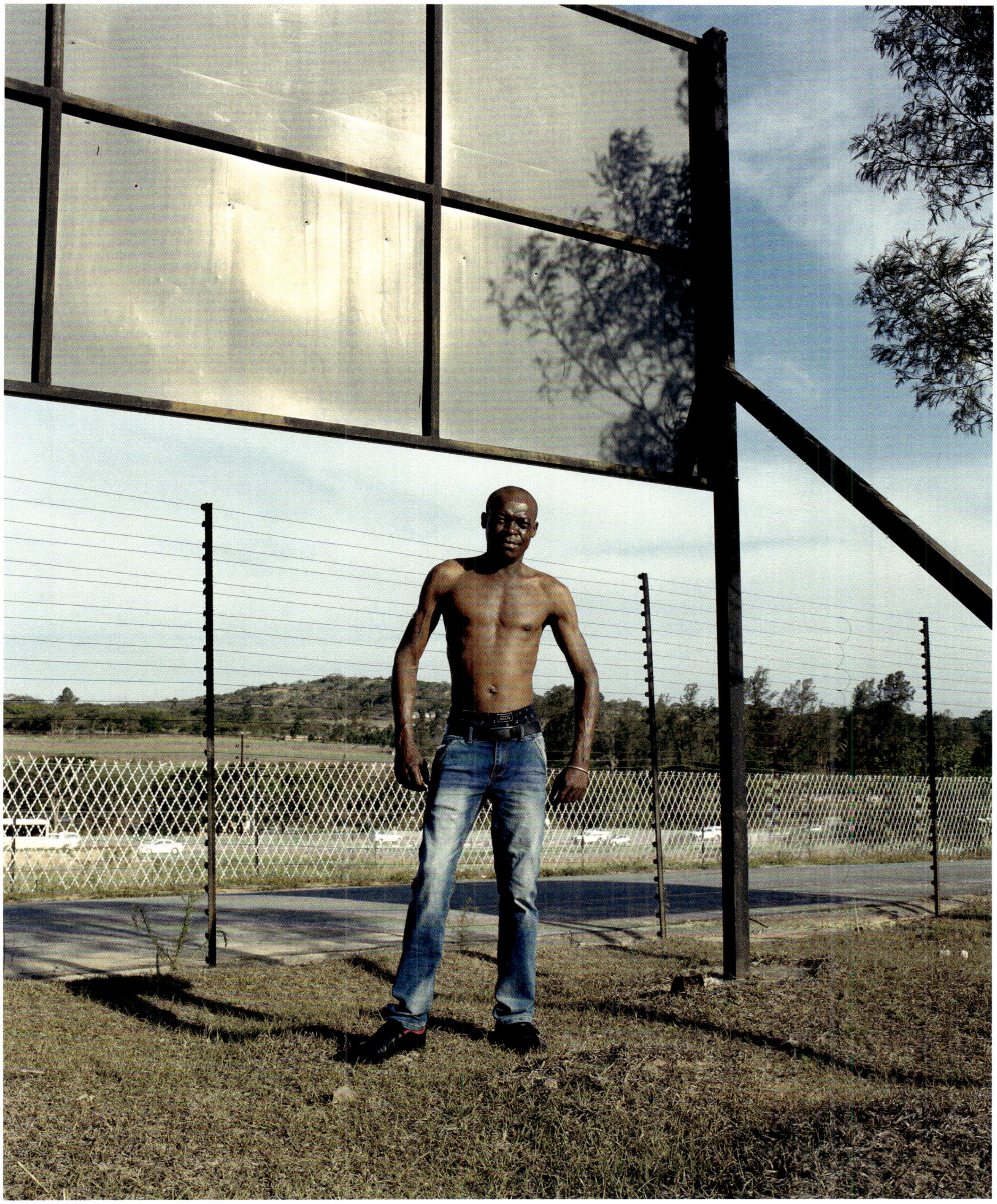

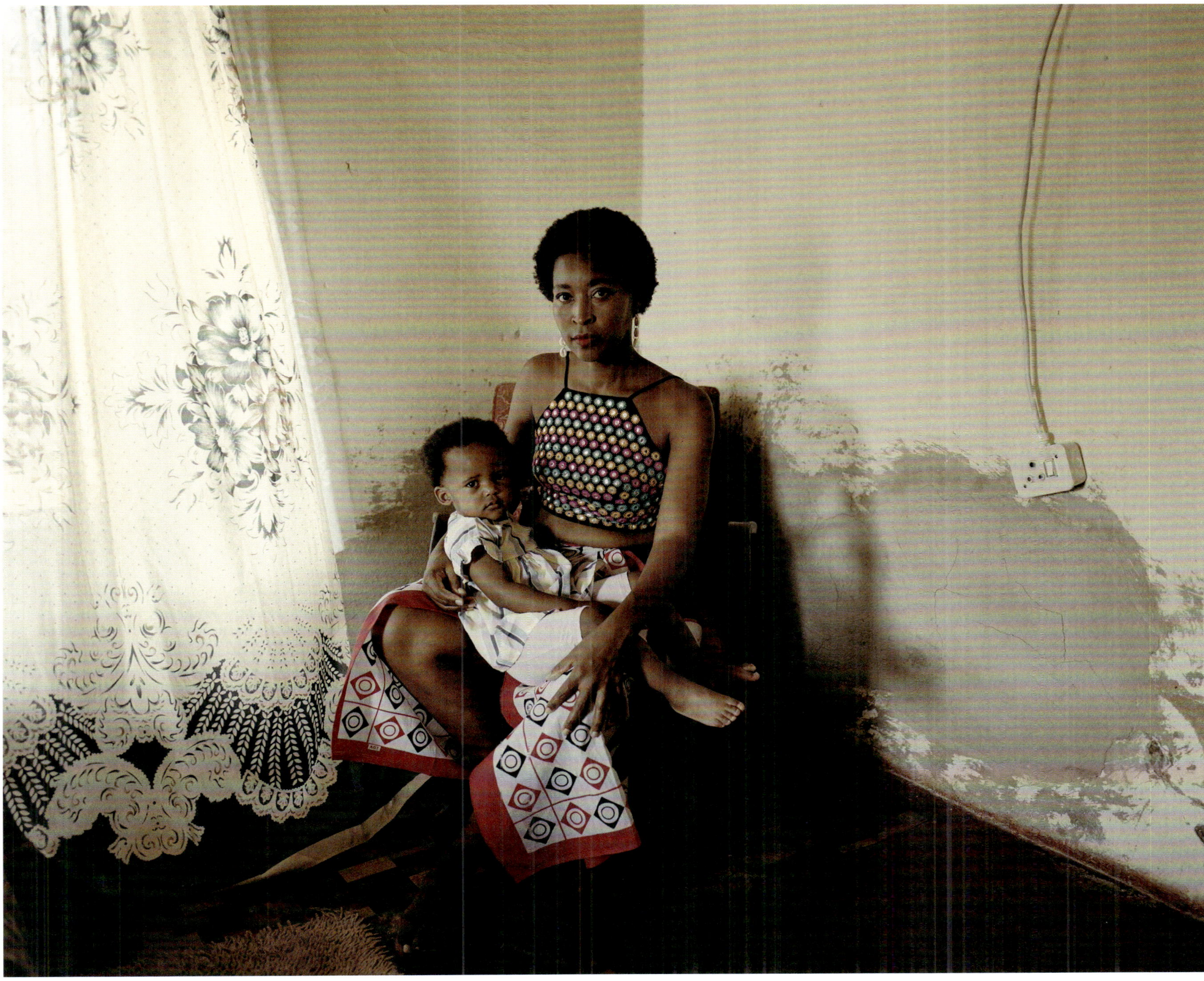

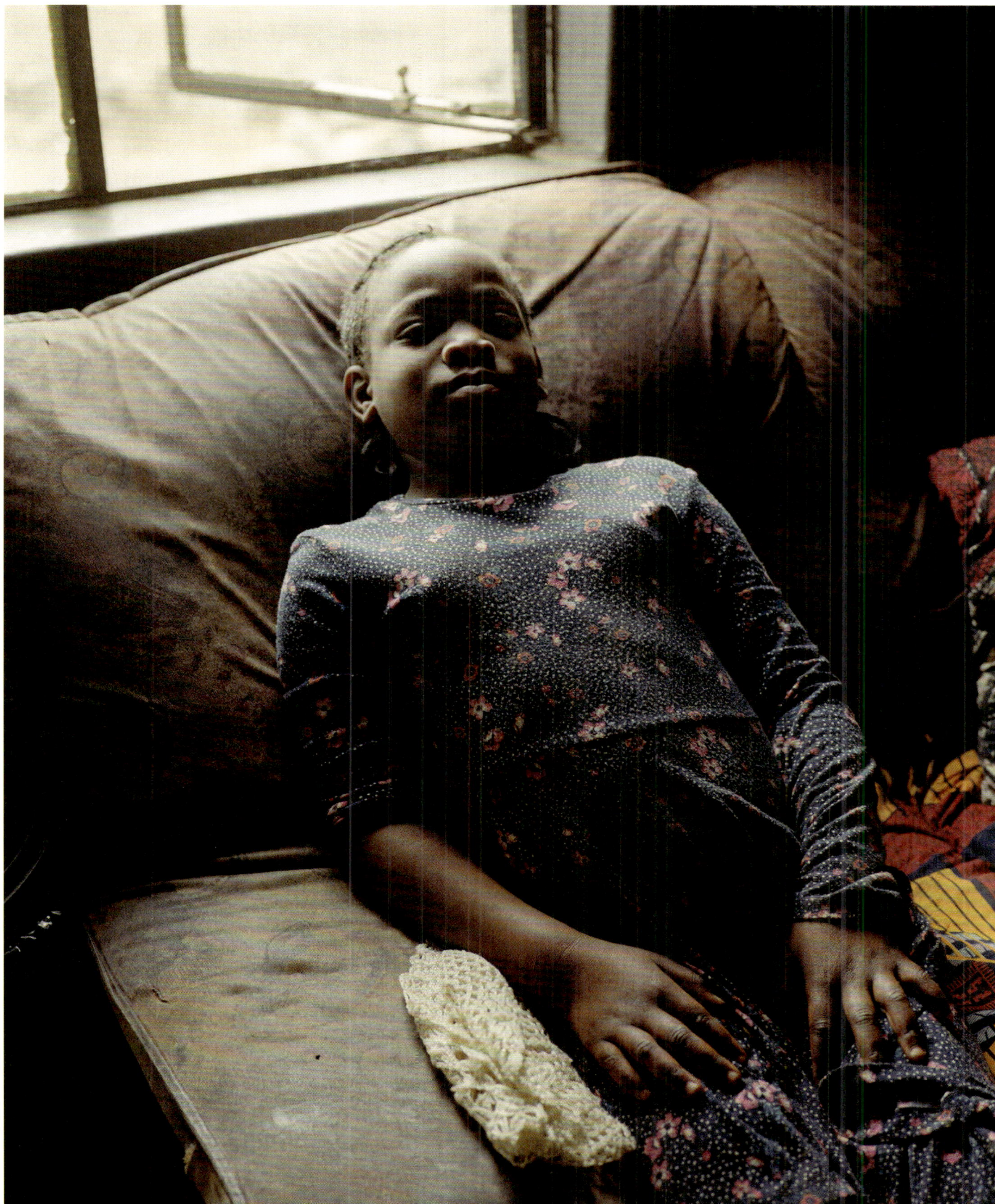

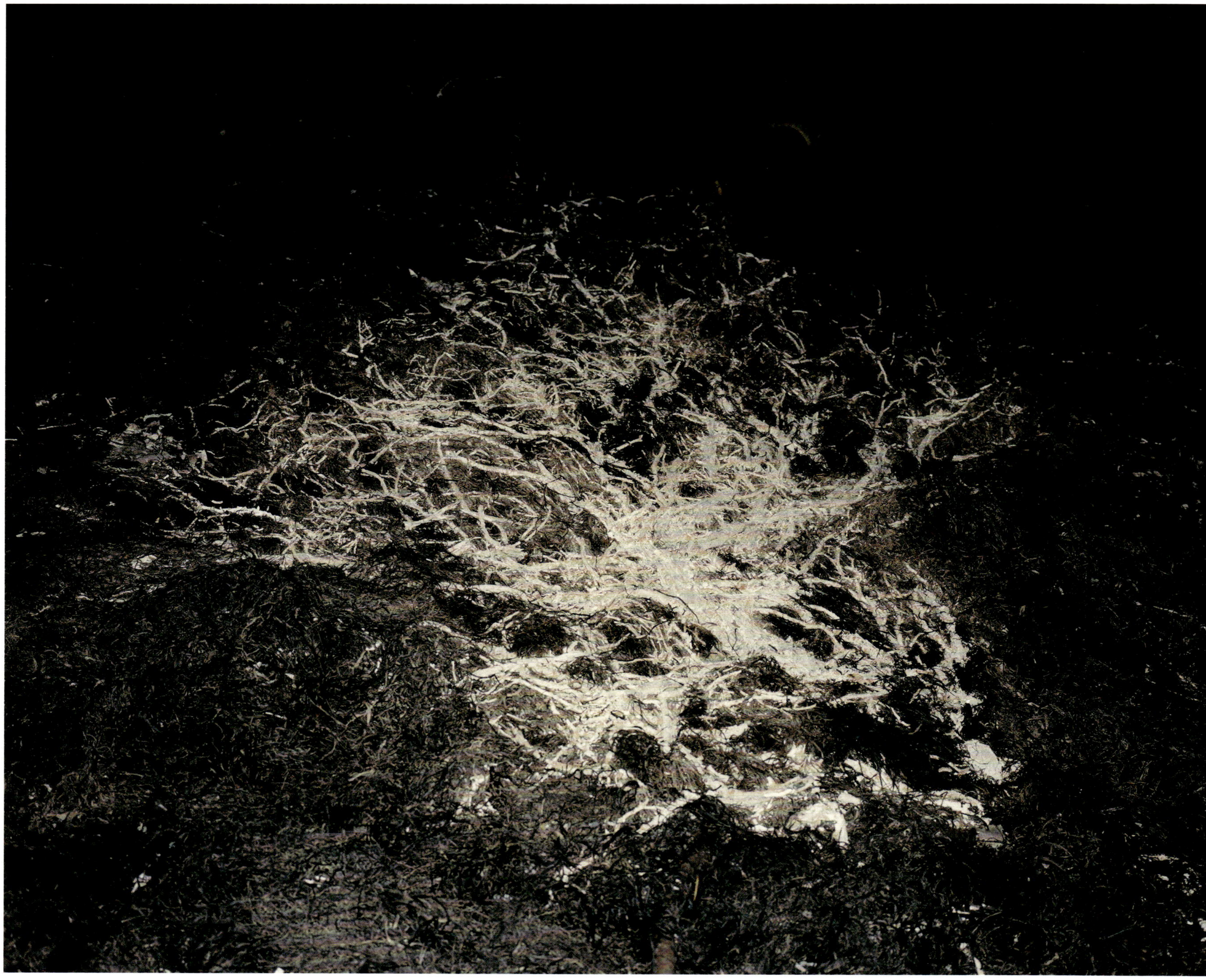

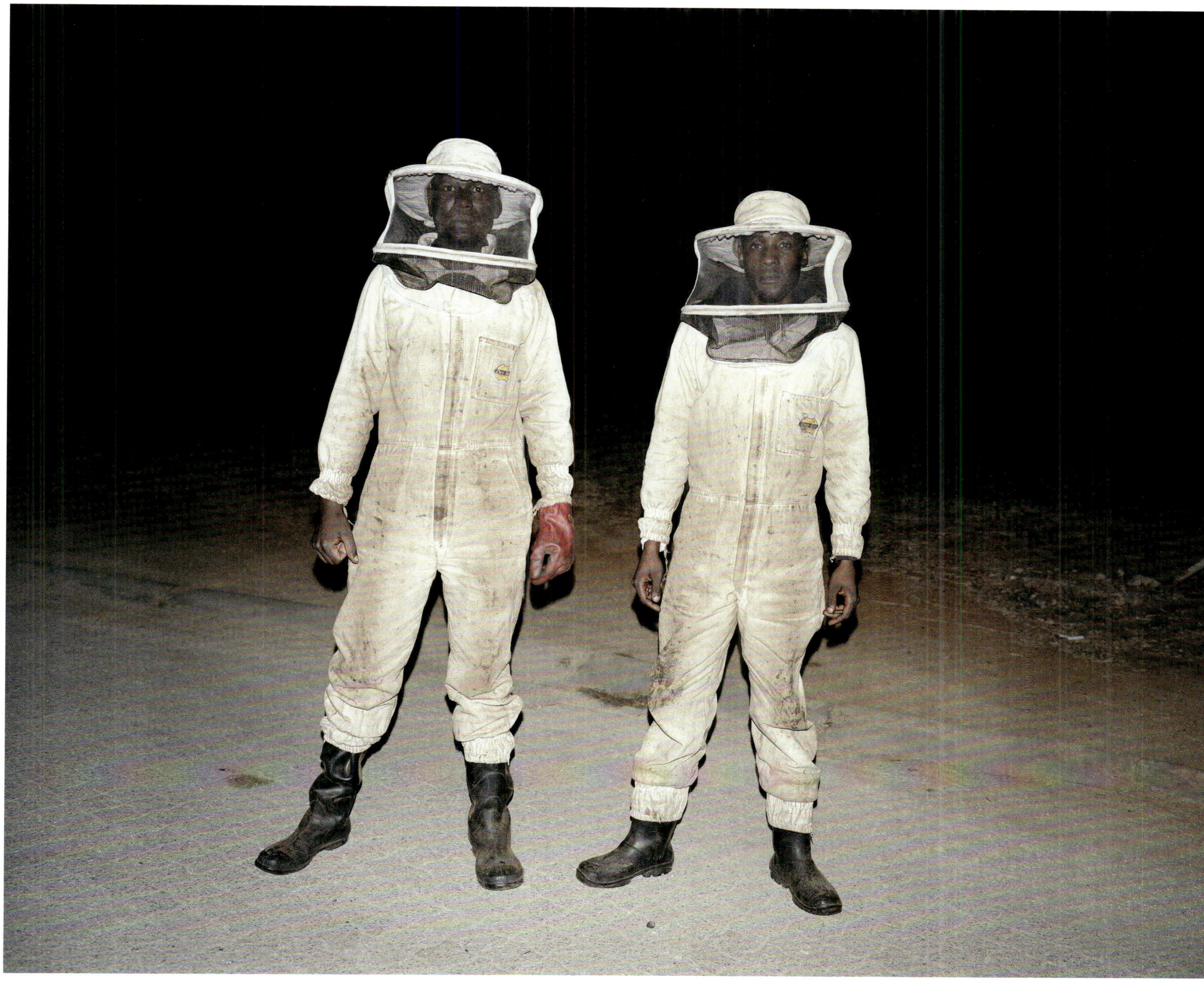

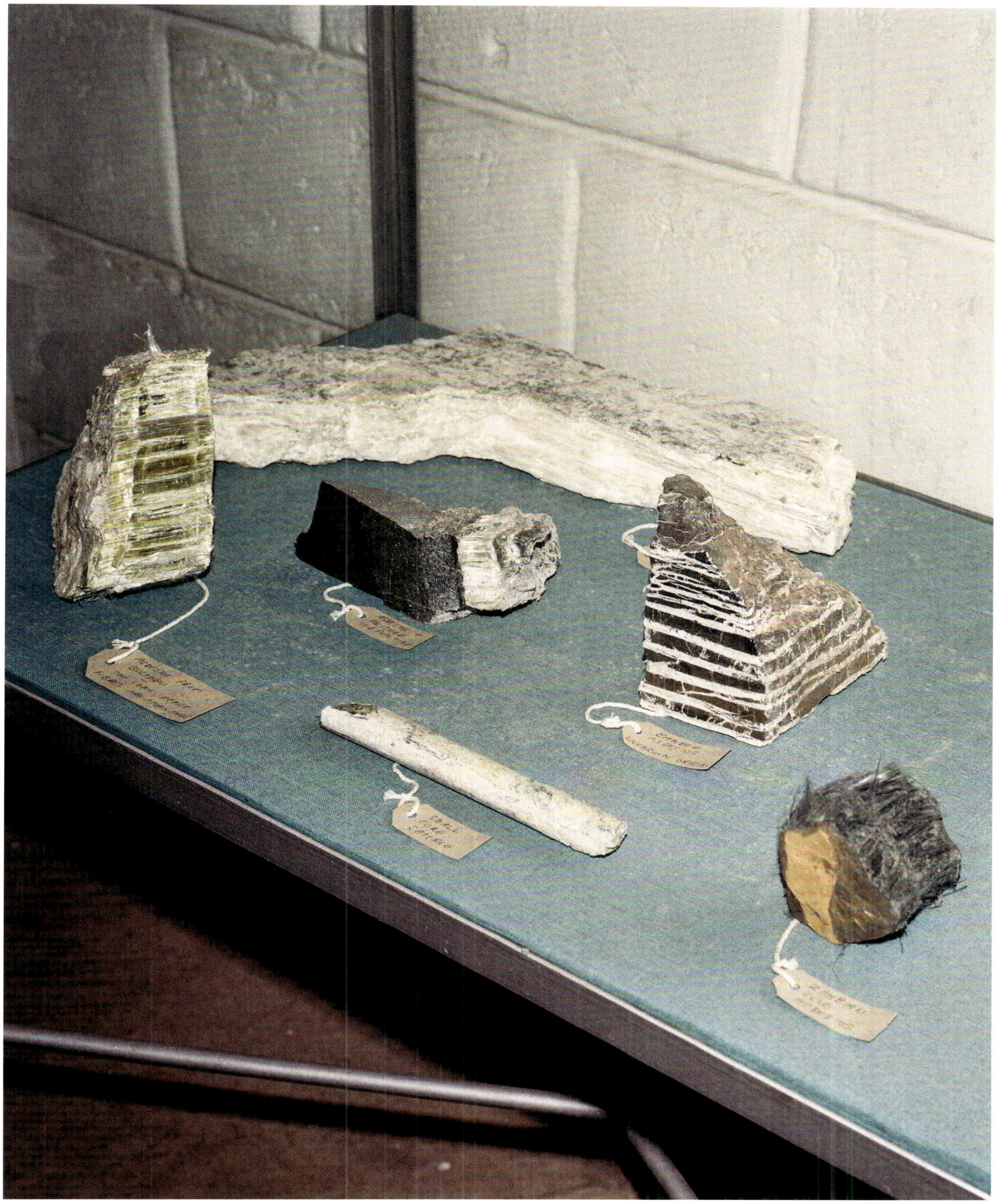

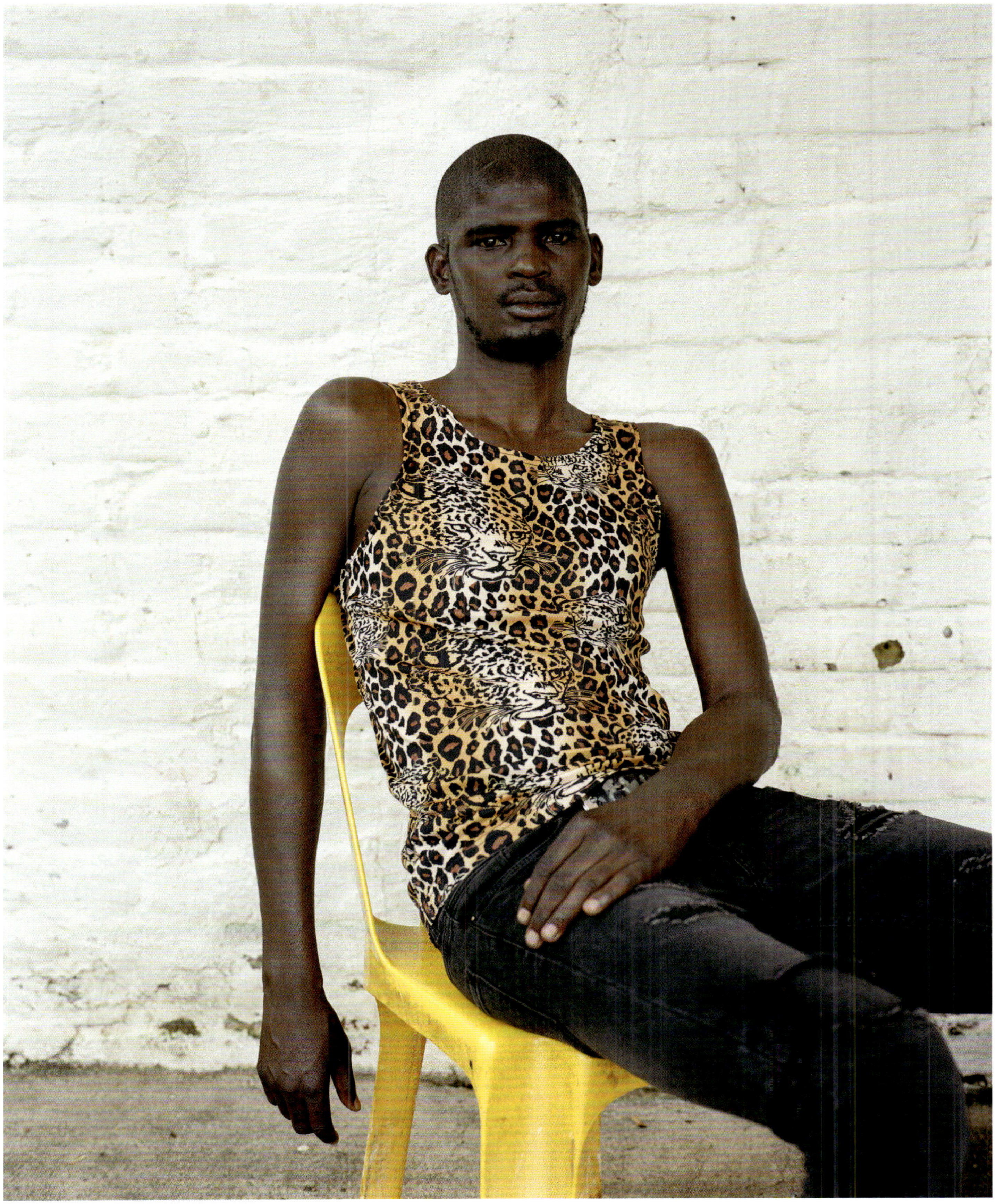

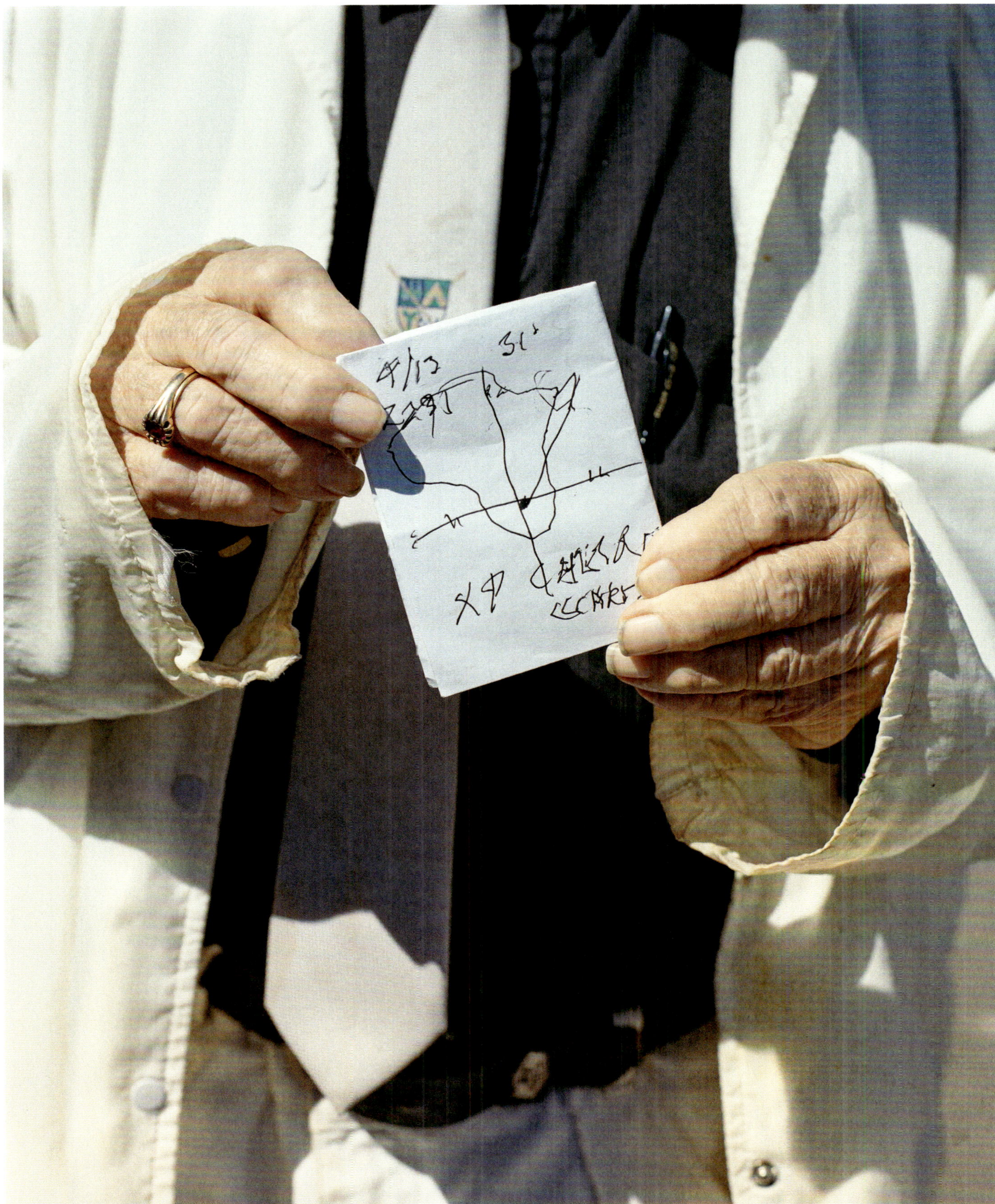

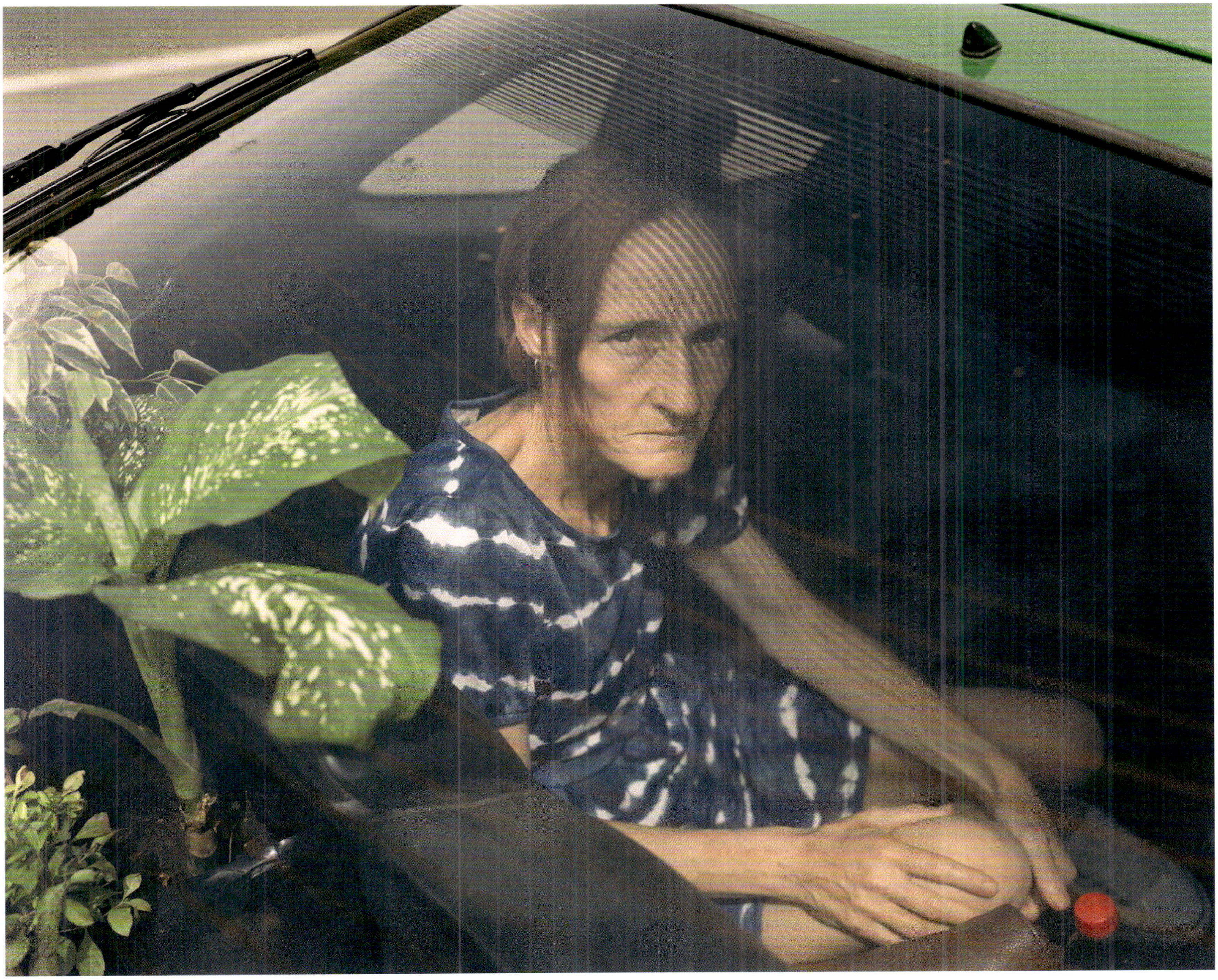

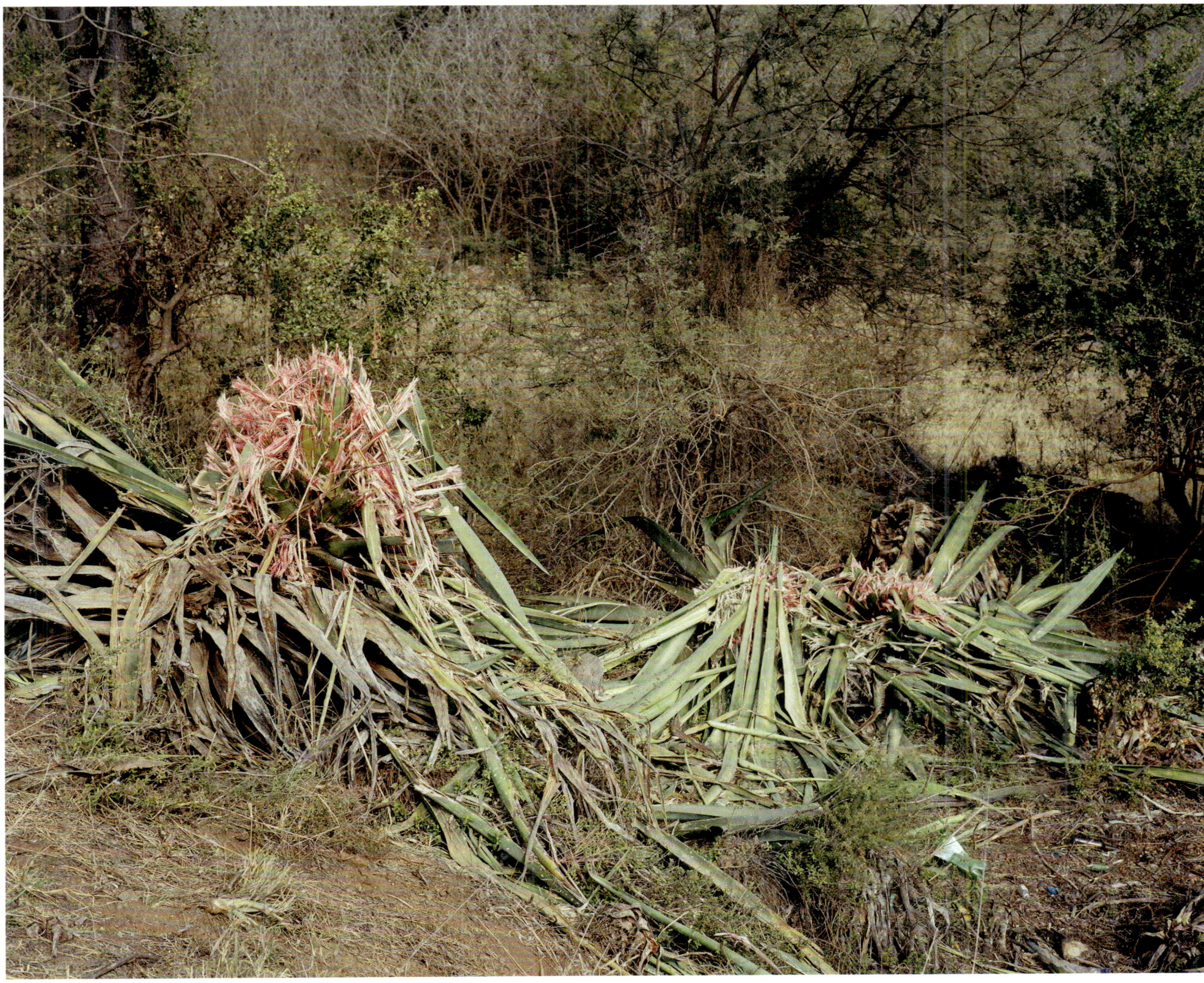

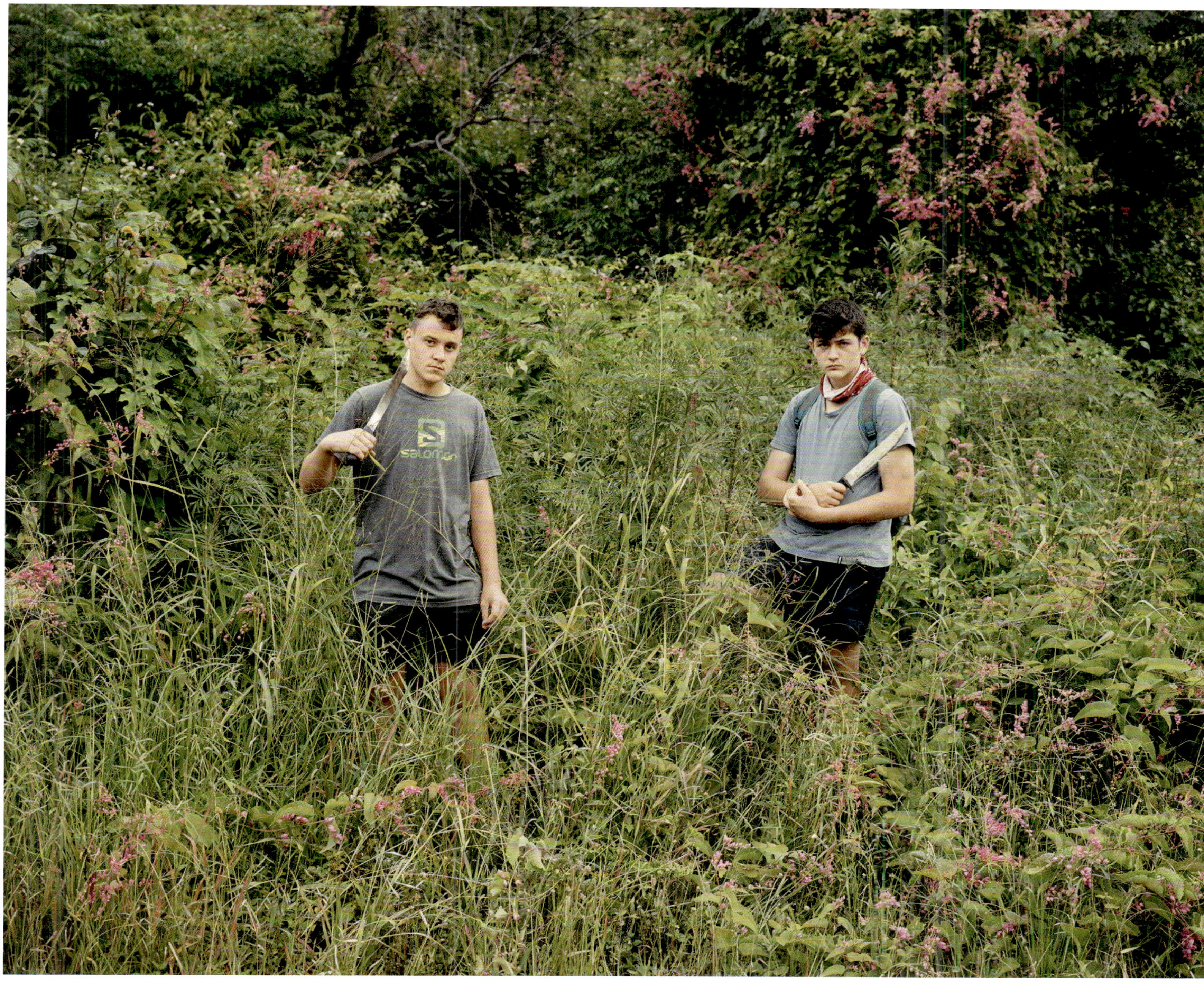
salomon

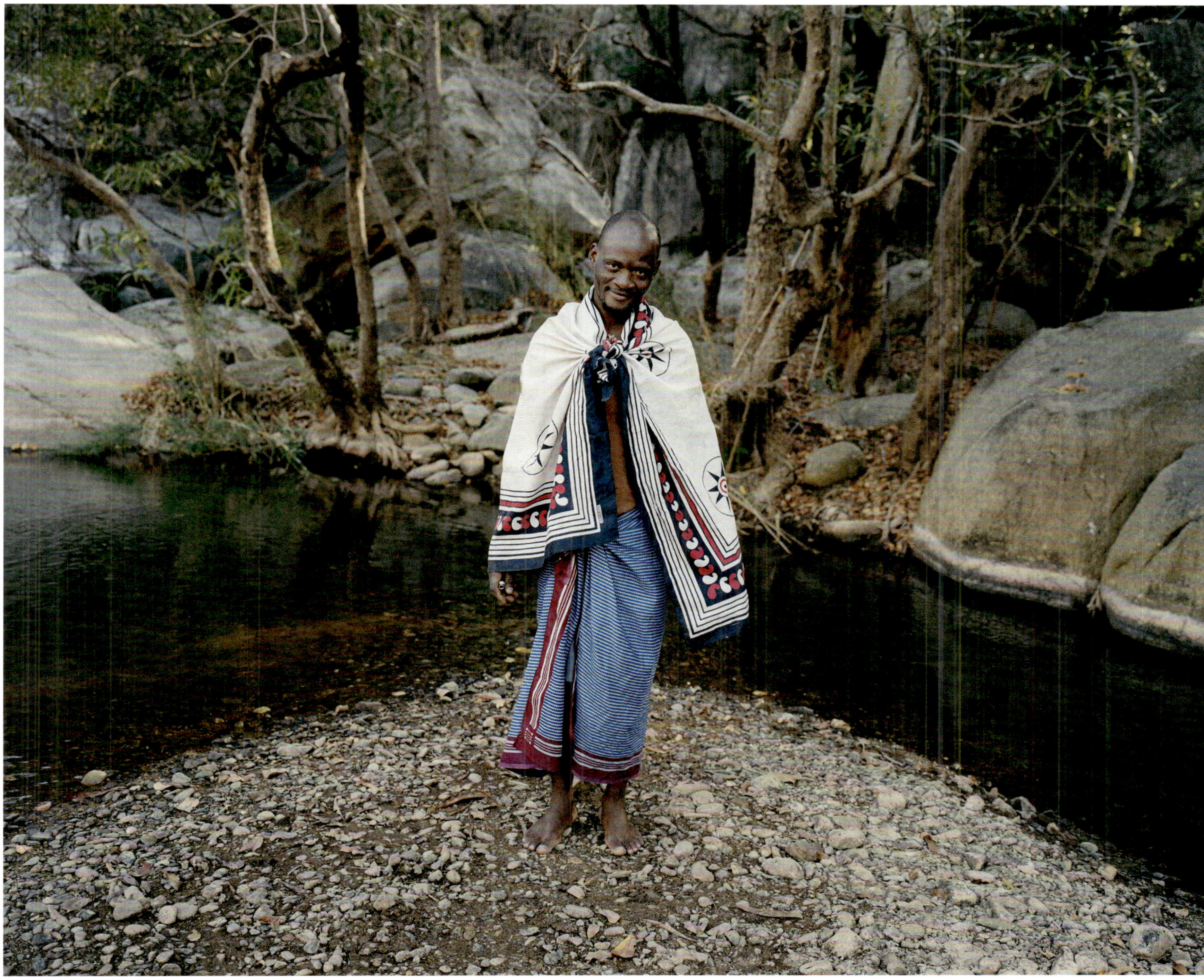

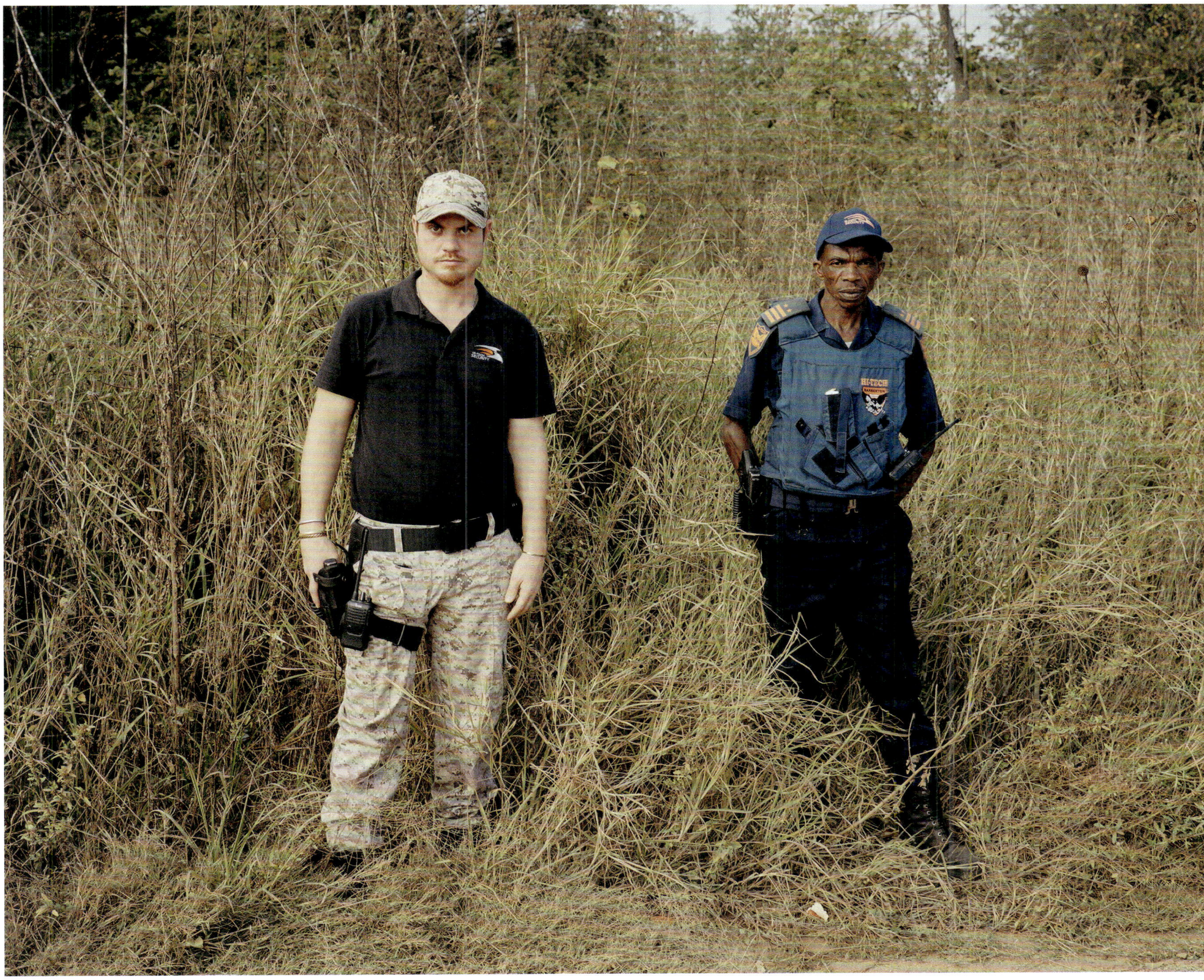

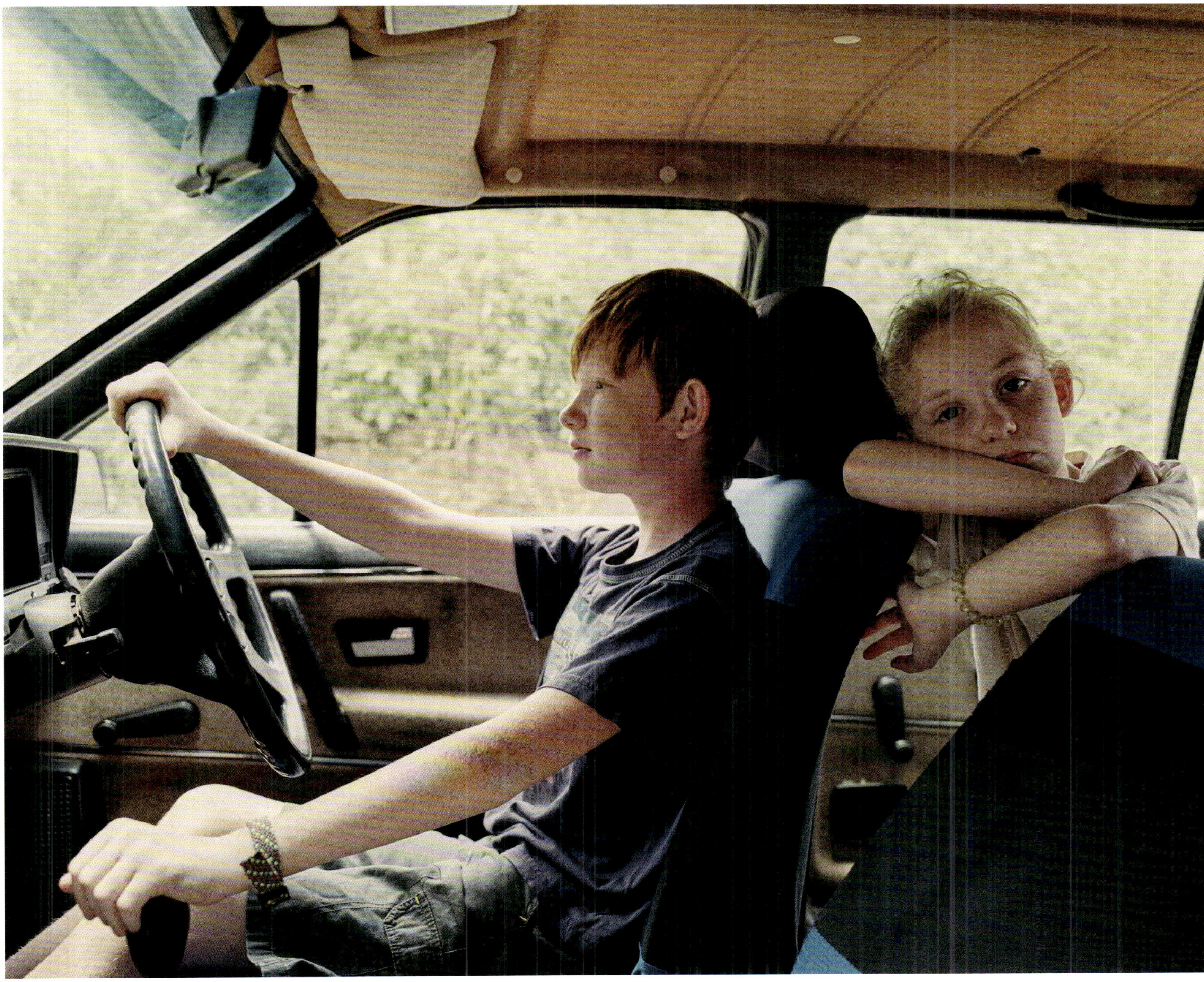

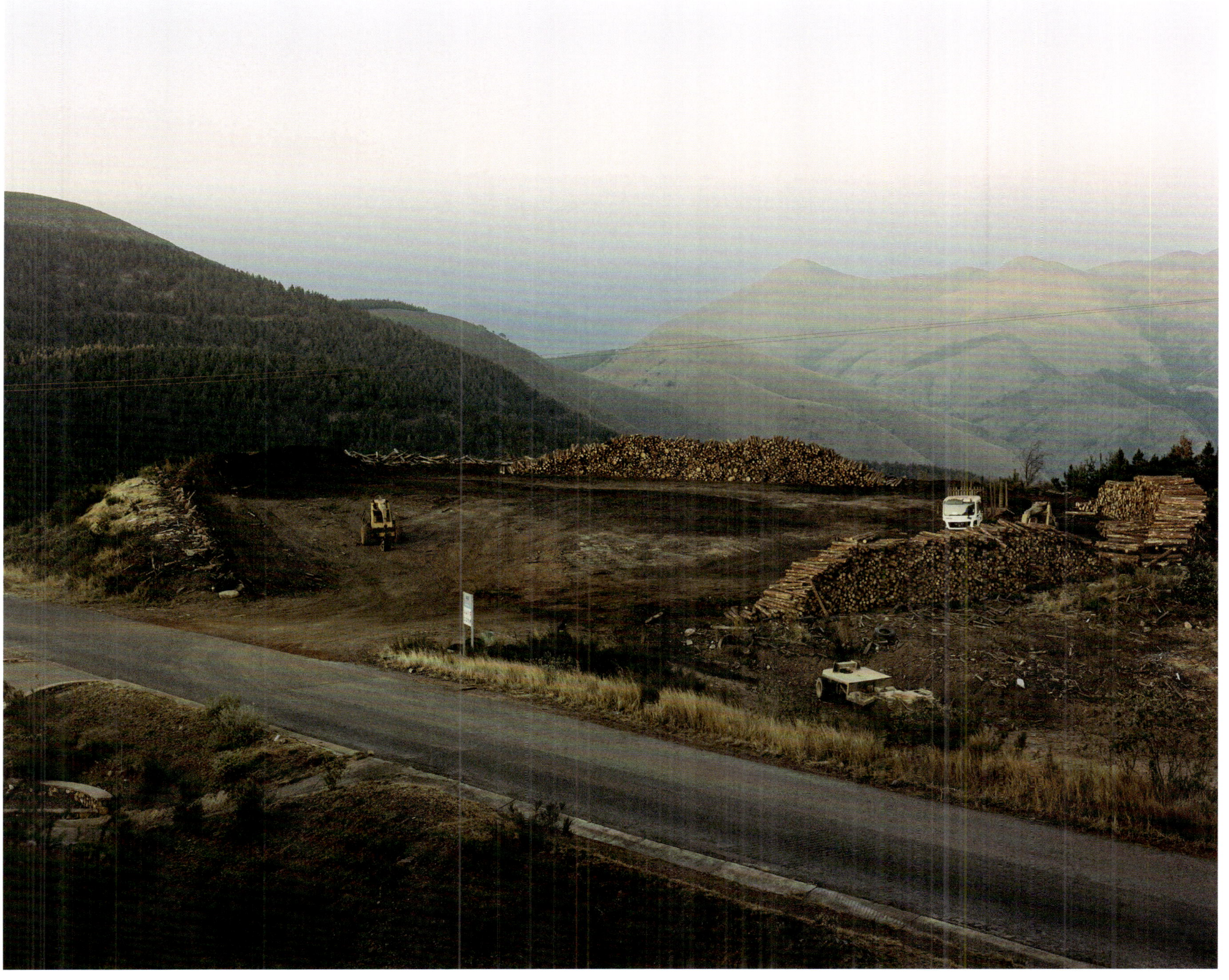

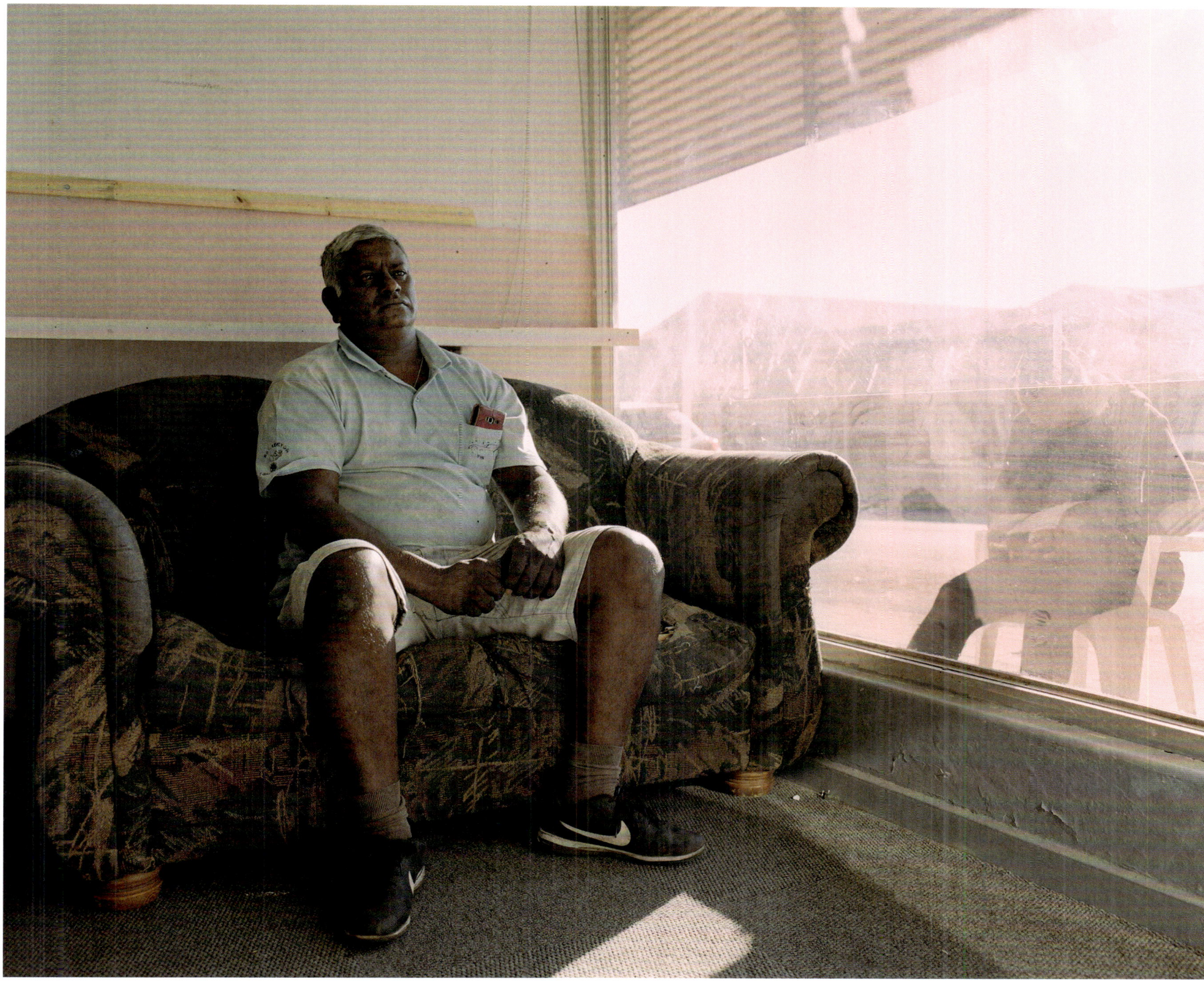

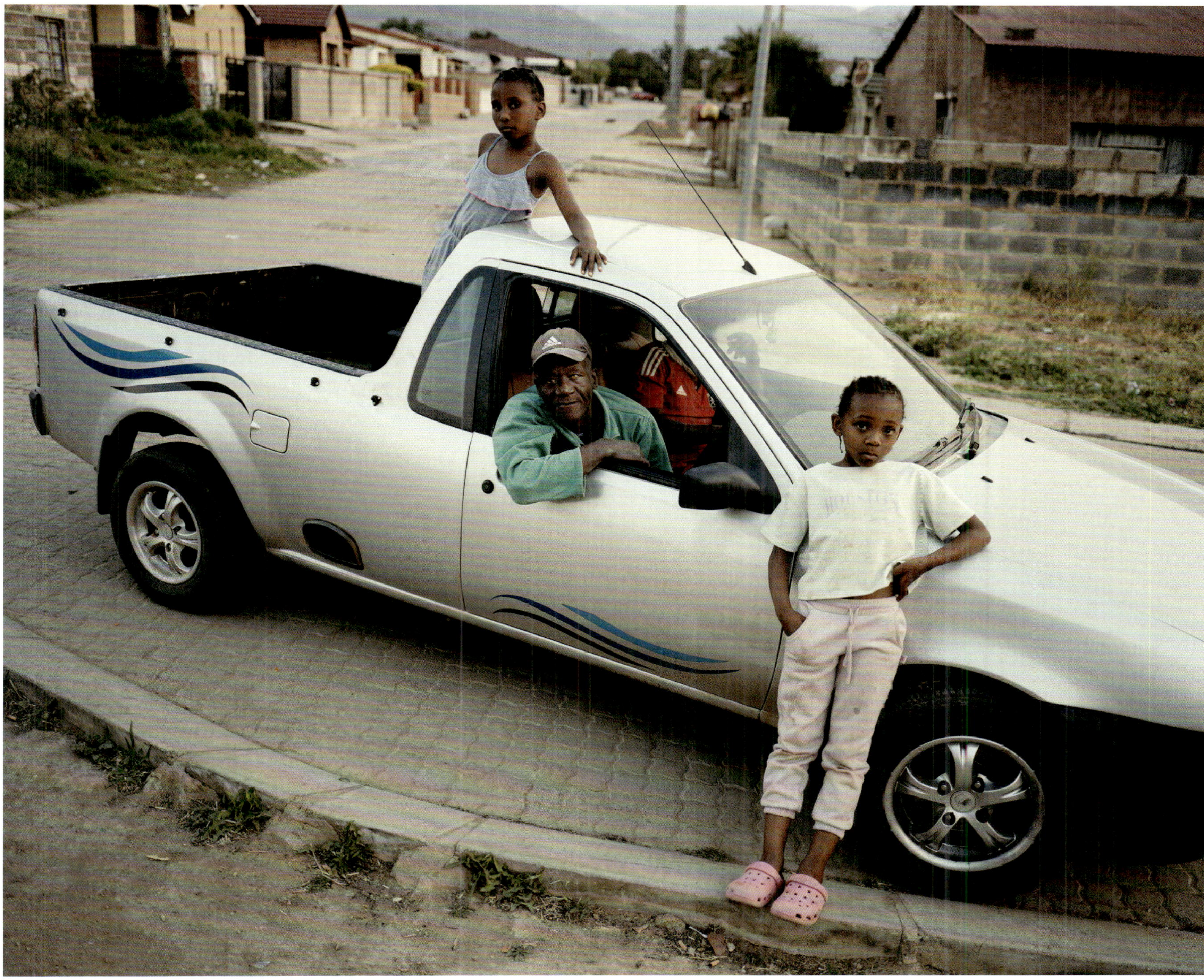

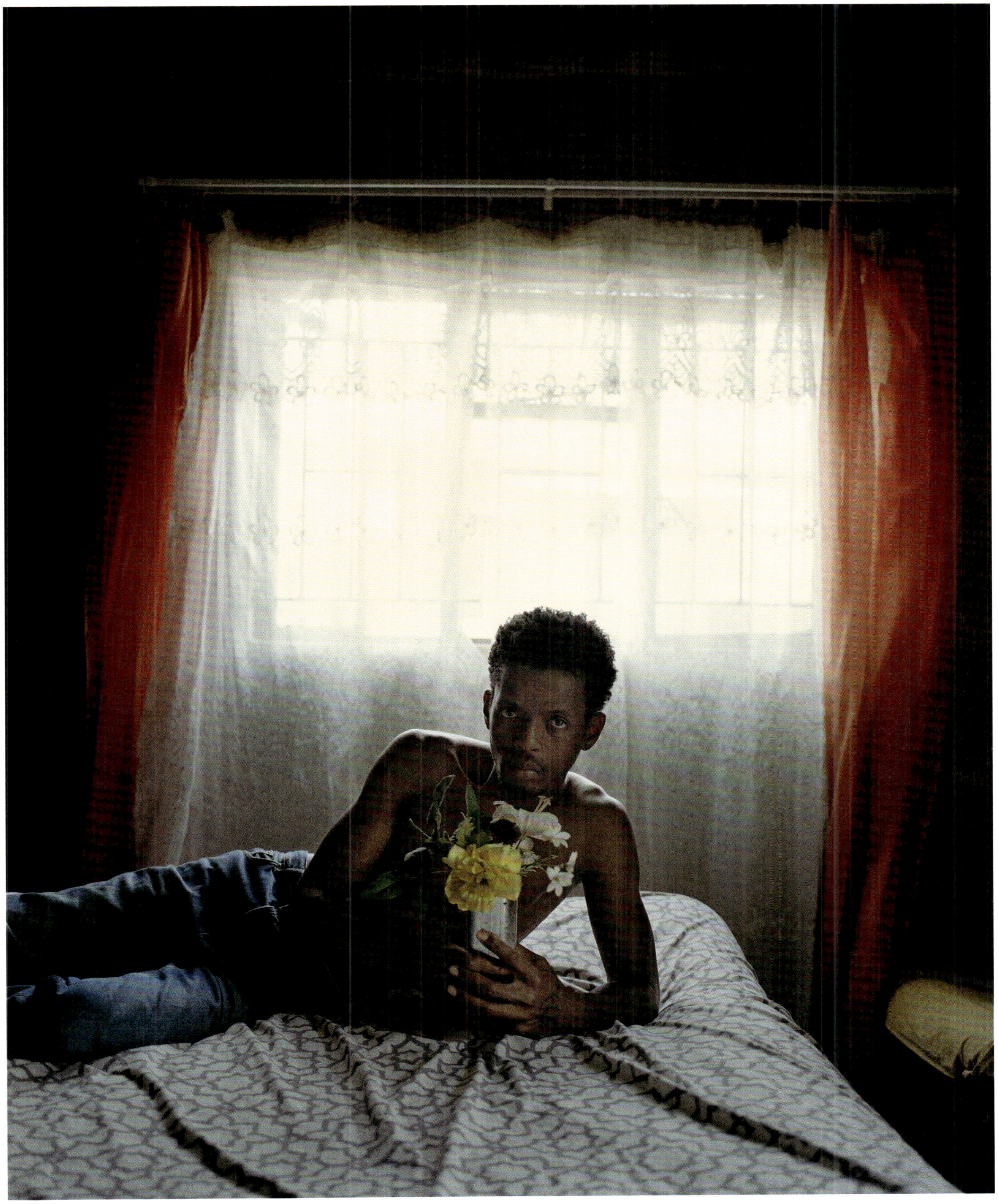

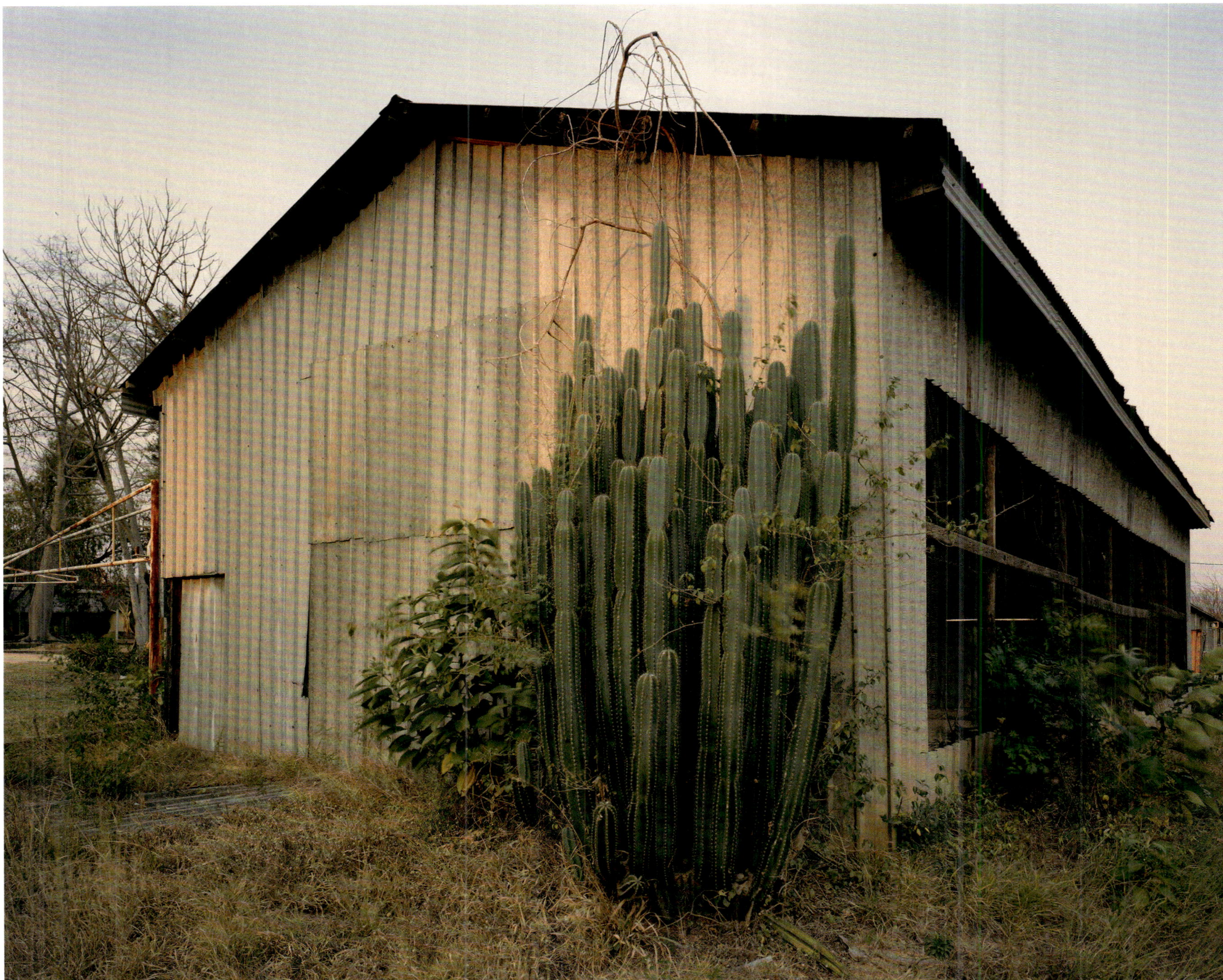

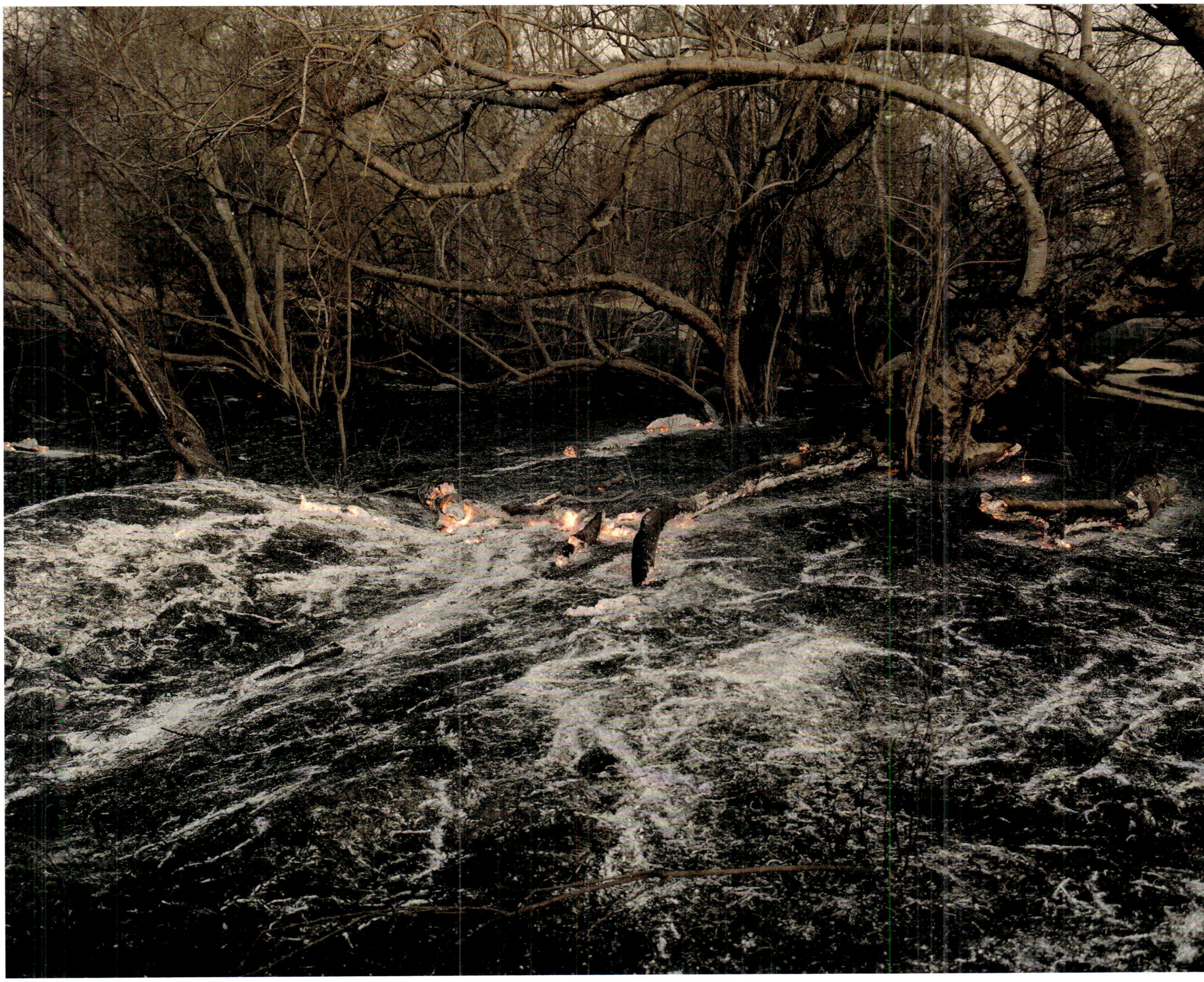

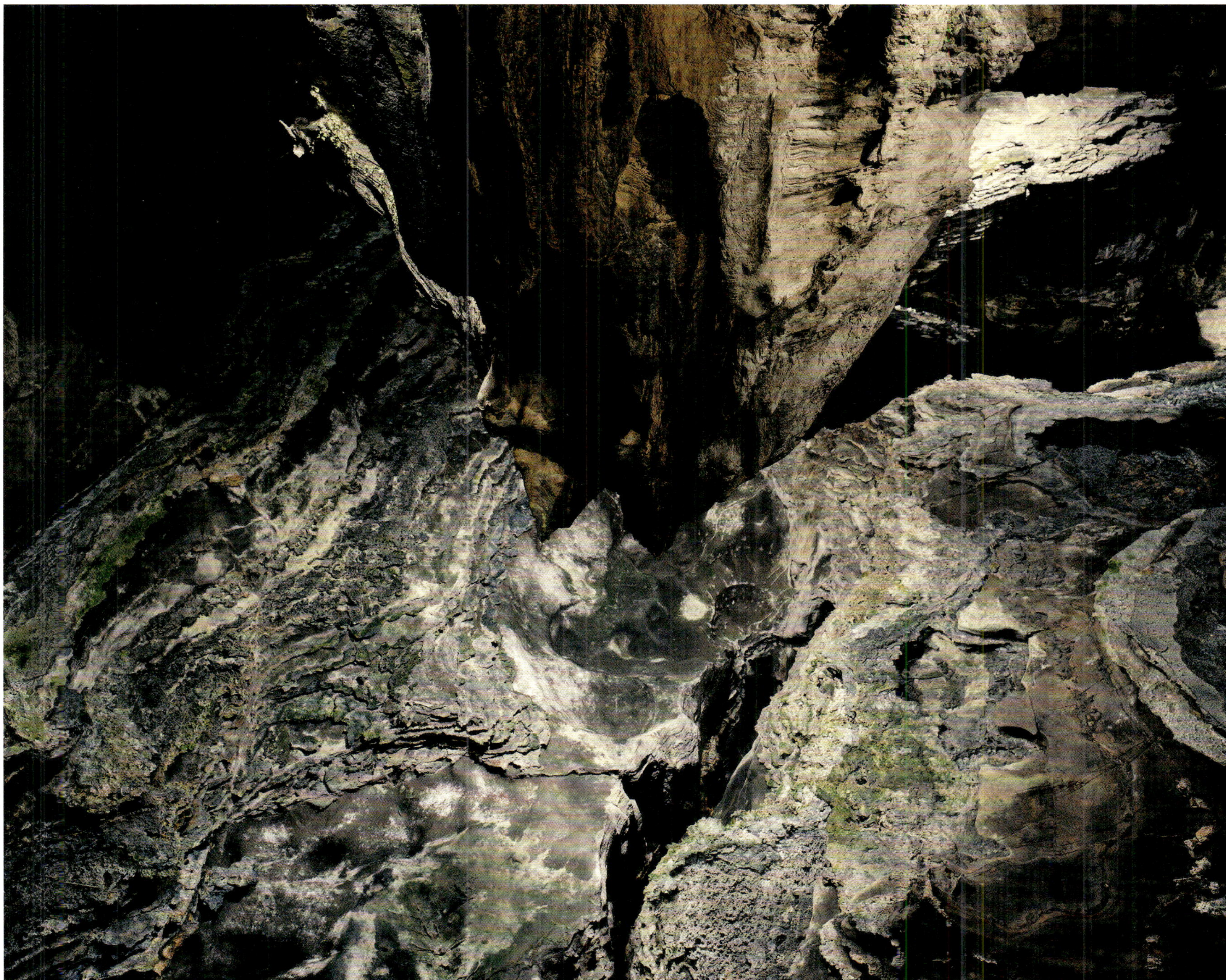

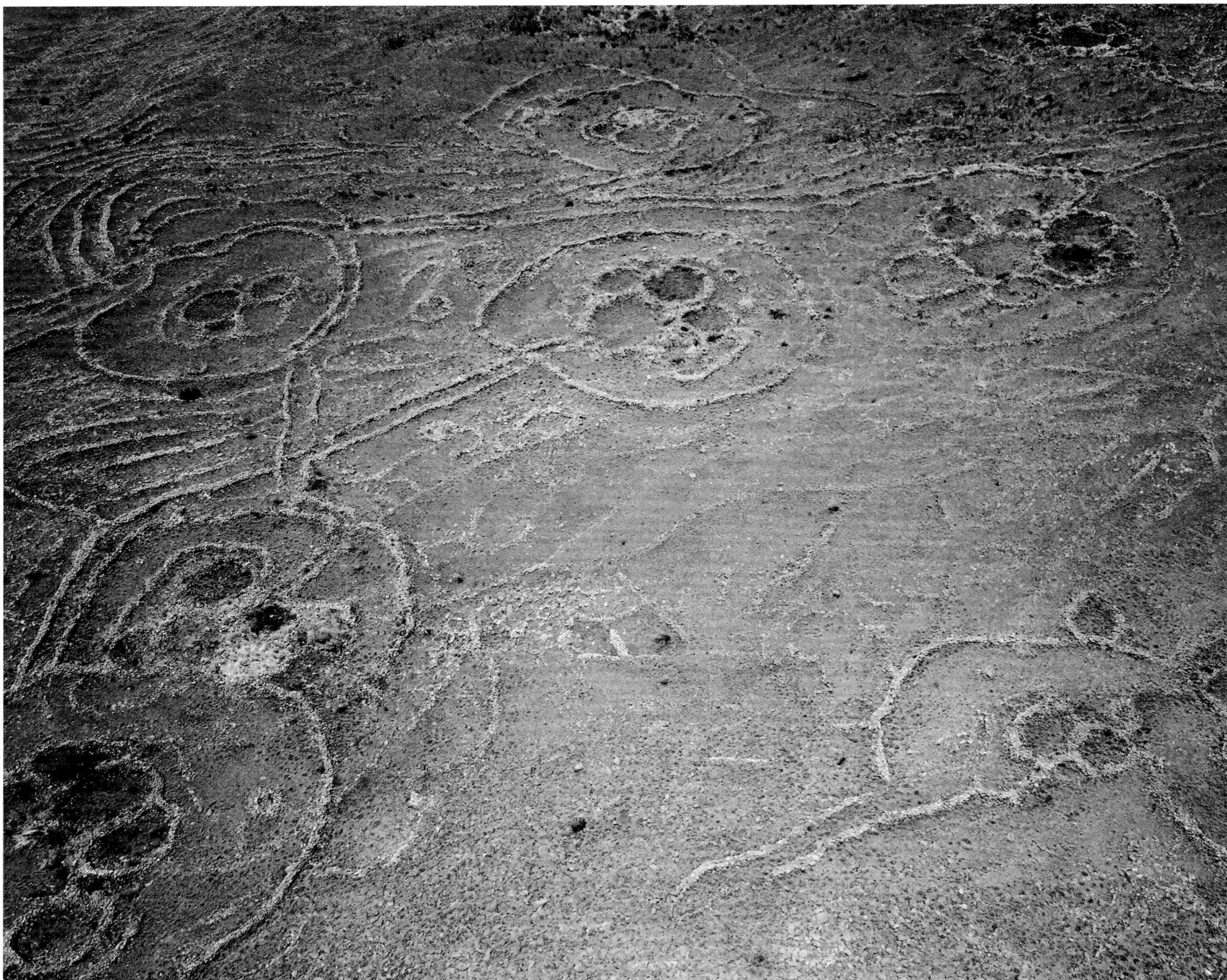

A BOY WHO IS MADE OF STONE

Up here, amidst the forest, in this pervasive silence, in this dense fog, a large stone structure occupies the landscape. To get here, one drives up a dirt road, along planted trees and then the road abruptly comes to an end, along a steel gate. The stones are layered in multiple shapes. Arbitrary lines. Careful stacking. Uneven sizing. From one angle, it looks like a kraal, with an entrance and an exit but then from another angle, the entrance and exit are just collapsed rocks. The rocks are tightly stacked atop of one another so that they can only be taken apart by meticulously removing them from the top down. The silence is deafening up here, but every now and then, people hear a song being hummed, which falls to a dead silence when they try to listen carefully. A voice that wants to sing but not be listened to. The locals have convinced one another that someone lives up on the mountains by the stones.

One morning, terrified children emerge from the forest by the black stone structure. They tumble down the mountain, into their homes, screaming that a boy made of thin, black stone is chasing after them.

The humming is Stone Boy.

'He has long arms. No, he has short arms. He has a limp. He was wearing one shoe.' The children argue.

There is only one detail the children agree on. They tried to hit the boy with stones, and the stones rebounded and the sound echoed through the forest.

The adults listen with haunted faces and knowing nods. This is the first time that Stone Boy is seen. Before, only the humming was heard, and on one occasion someone had heard the thudding sound of footsteps amongst the trees.

Later that day, the men meet away from the wives and children to discuss what the children have said about Stone Boy. Up on the main road, by the hollow highway tunnel, the men gather in a circle and collude. Something unspoken and mystical hangs about their presence. They have heard stories about this from their great grandparents.

'At last, Stone Boy has been spotted,' someone breaks the silence.

'If it is him,' another old man counters.

This is heavy and they look out into the sunset glistening on the scarred landscape—heaps of earth, dug up for minerals, abandoned, and now only talked about with disdain.

'This was always going to happen. He was always going to return home. Stone Boy is the child of this place,' a man chimes in with a stutter.

'It's been so many years now. Surely, this isn't him,' one of the men in the gathering says.

'But what about what the children saw. Are they lying?' another asks.

Many years ago, Stone Boy, then thirteen, climbed up a mountain and stepped into a bucket on the forty-kilometre-long cableway that carried minerals from the mines into the processing plants. The cableway lost power, and he was stuck, way too high above the mountain, above the stacked black stones. He jumped off over the black stones, mistaking them for soft black soil. And now he is stone.

There's history here, violently folded into the exploited landscape, the inaccessible closed mines, the visible damage on the earth.

When the children return from the mountain,

claiming a boy made of stone chased after them, the adults know exactly what they are talking about, even though they dismiss the children. Histories don't get erased because people don't speak about them. In fact, in the silence, violent histories turn into legacies in the memory of others.

The sun fully disappears behind the hills before the men can conclude their discussion. In a short time, one by one, each hill, each mound, disappears into the darkness. At night, the landscape turns into myth, a vacuum into an already shifting mining history. The men follow the flickering light of the torch to their homes. They arrive in their houses and find their wives sitting up and armed with an ammunition of questions on the tip of their tongues. The children pretend to be asleep under the blankets, their bodies all covered, but they leave their ears outside the blankets. Under the cover of night, the men tell the ancient truth of Stone Boy, because this story is only told in the dark, away from uninvited ears. It is a story passed down from their great grandparents.

The wives hear a cautionary tale, and the children, staying still and attentive under the blankets, hear magic. In the days after, children gather in street corners and entertain one another with their versions of the same story. They all heard their fathers telling their mothers and yet their recalling of the stories about Stone Boy is vastly different. The details of the story are at the mercy of their remembering and retelling. In their version of the story, land contours shift, tree plantations run wild, weird creatures emerge from hidden gulfs. Each parent tries to reprimand their child at home, to warn them off the stories, to reel them back from their invented fantasies, but imagination is the source of life for children. Besides, by then it is too late, the children have added their own magic to the Stone Boy story, and to them it is now true.

The day Stone Boy disappeared, his mother watched him run down the road and disappear into the park. As the hours passed, and he did not return home, she ran in panic into the street, a mad woman who had misplaced her son. She rounded up all of his friends, rummaged through their homes, and found nothing. An innocent search turned into delusion in a single afternoon. Her grief was immediate. She made his bed the way he liked it, pillows laid horizontally, blanket folded at the bottom, carpets fully inserted underneath the bed. He liked the cold feeling underneath his feet in the morning when he got out of bed and stepped onto the bare floor. 'In case Melokuhle comes back,' She justified it to her husband.

In the mornings, she inspected if the bed was slept in, and each morning, she was overwhelmed with disappointment. And then she waited outside every day, in the chair underneath the tree by the front gate, in case he came back home. Her husband walked past her every day from work and eventually stopped loving her. Everyone heard about this and there were murmurs about her mad behaviour. There were jokes about how this Melokuhle she was waiting for had always been a strange child anyway, always talking to himself, in animated gestures, instead of having real friends like other children.

She searched for him everywhere. Her own backyard, the neighbours, the abandoned town hall, and then far out into the landscape. Her search started in the highveld and descended into the lowveld. Thin air and thick air moving through her pained heart. She walked the growing weeds, carefully planted trees, charred plantations, steep escarpments. A land with fluctuating identities. Her search came out empty. She found only the heavy heart she now keeps inside her chest.

Years go by and she gives birth to a girl, Angel, trying to get close to her husband after they drift apart. The reprieve is fleeting. When Angel is born, she tells her everything about Melokuhle. She paints a complete family portrait. This angers her husband, and he spends nights away from home. She spends those nights soaking the pillow with tears. On one of the rare nights that her husband is home, she wakes him up, in panic. 'Melokuhle is in the kitchen burning pap like he always did,' she says to him. There was pap burning but nobody was there. 'You just forgot to put the coals out,' he simply mumbles in bed, unbothered to get up.

Another day, she wakes up from an afternoon nap sweating from a nightmare. In it, everything is on fire, but it is pouring outside, and wet grass doesn't burn. A few hours later, just after sunset, with the rain still pouring, the landscape catches fire. The locals map the fire to the asbestos mine, not far from where Stone Boy was last seen. Melokuhle's mother is convinced that it was her son.

'He's scorching the earth because we won't go get him,' she says to the gathered crowd.

The landscape turns red from the flames, and it becomes a myth. The fire drifts across it, creeping further up, until it disappears, only the red sky telling of the unseen flames. Fire and rain at the same time. It leaves everyone perplexed.

On the vast landscape, sometimes an explosion is heard, illegal miners digging out the insides of the mountain for leftover gold. The rumble can go on for the whole day. If you listen carefully, it sounds like something menacing is crawling out of the mountains, and once it is out, it'll swallow the community in one mouthful.

The churches etched up to the side of the mountain mistake the rumble for the second coming of Jesus. The word of God spreads everywhere here, into the seams of the locals, so they can take it everywhere they go. Or not go. There is a running joke here, that they know that one is from here because they have never left. An unlucky town. First, its beautiful landscapes are dug out for mineral wealth, and then it is left abandoned. Exploited and unusable.

Along the ruins, once the mines close, toxic water gathers gold dust as it flows down on the side of the mountain, past the houses over the bridge, into the streams that hug the bottom of the sloping land. By the bridge, passing cars pull over to the side, to the echoes of traffic, and look down into the river, where the glittering water flows down the mountain, collecting gold residue on its way.

Stone Boy becomes a 'Zama Zama' in his adolescent years. Because he's made of stone, he digs through rocks with his bare hands. Gold residue is stuck underneath his fingernails. But there is nothing left here. Prospectors from the past dug up everything, melted it into gold coins and left. There is only despair and there is a lot of it and sometimes people kill each other because of it.

Stone Boy disappears into the abandoned mines for months. He doesn't see the sun. He misses the thunderstorms. Mineshafts extend far, and on some of the days, he digs underneath his own mother's house. His mother tosses and turns in bed, longing for a son who is an arm-stretch away, beneath the ground, in a dark, tight, tunnel. When he comes above ground, Stone Boy finds a shifting world. Entire populations are disappearing. He finds fading childhood memories on the demolished mine compounds, their footsteps on the foundations. and doodles on the walls.

In all the years of his unknown whereabouts, Stone Boy's mother came close to finding him only once, in a place called Inzalo Ye Langa, the birthplace of the sun, where people gather to welcome the new year. A footprint and flattened grass are seen. But she is the only one who believes it. Everyone still thinks she is mad. A hoping mother is a mad mother. And indeed, her brain atrophies and then on one of her searches for her boy she disappears. The husband burns her belongings and marries again. Only Stone Boy mourns his mother.

The landscape catches fire at an alarming rate. Mountain tops ignite one after the other. Livestock starves. Plantations burn to the ground. Nobody can explain it.

It has taken years for Stone Boy to be spotted on the mountain. Each generation has carried its own stories of him, each with equal doubt and belief. The elders wonder if he now wants to come home—that he chased after the children because perhaps he is exhausted of roaming the landscape and they are the only ones who will believe in him and tell of their encounter with absolute conviction and zero doubt.

Lidudumalingani

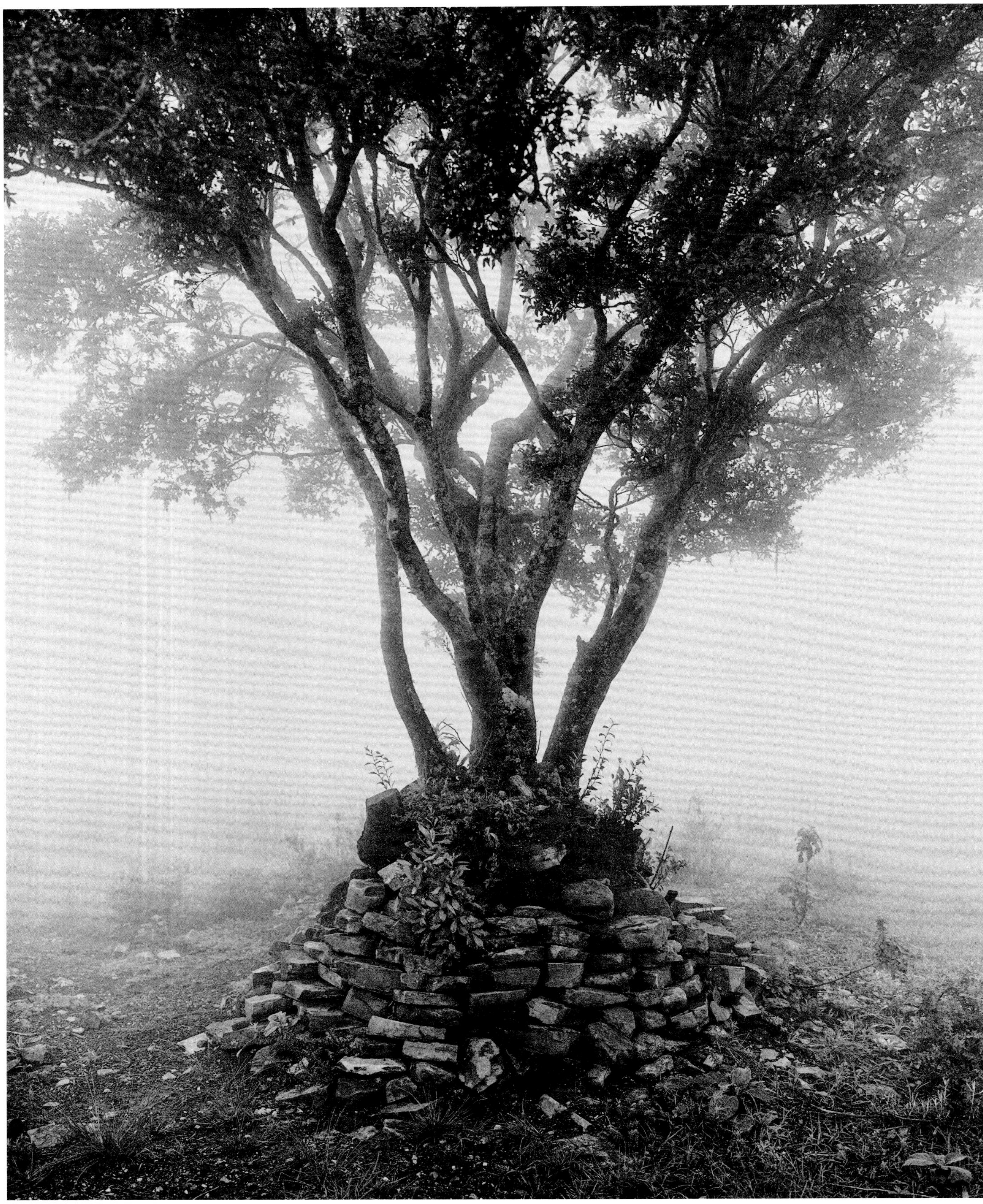

EPILOGUE

Wind and altitude shape our senses, bringing the timbre of the land to our awareness. *Mapalakata.* It sounds as though it comes from the east, carried on the same currents that squeeze weather up against the escarpment. The syllables move like traders once did, deliberately, following rivers that fall from the plateau to the coast. Salt left its crystals in their bags and stained their robes, and the copper and iron they brought left their colours on their palms.

The terrain holds evidence of passage. A footpath pressed into dolerite. A shard of glass where basalt splits under heat. Water cutting a new course after rain. There is no memory in that, only record—matter shifted by contact and weather. Trucks climb the gradients where oxen once strained. Diesel smoke drifts across the grass where mica flickers under sun. The air tastes metallic at dawn, a trace of minerals drawn from stone. The escarpment rises sharply, the great inland shelf of Africa breaking into folded ridges. What lingers is not nostalgia but the accumulation of iron, pollen, ash, labour.

The name *Mapalakata* once meant traders. Men who came inland with cloth and beads, their packs heavy with salt and brass. They followed the flow of rivers, trading what they could carry for gold and hides and grain. The world they moved through was a web of bargains. Even now the region works with the same logic.

The trucks that grind up these roads are the new caravans, trailers groaning with timber, citrus, and coal. They leave a film of oil on the tar and a deep rhythm in the distance. Along the verges, workers walk home at dusk, the day's dust clinging to their sleeves. A farmer repairs a gate in the fading light. A woman sells fruit beside a petrol drum fire. They inhabit the future of history.

The high grasslands fold and unfold in brown cadence. Rivers plunge through gum forests and smoke trees, meandering into the lowveld heat. The smell of sap mixes with diesel and rain. Everything is in motion. The people do not stay still long enough to become statues.

Gold lies beneath them still, veins deep in the rock. The earth here is ancient, its age measured in billions of years. The Barberton Craton holds some of the earliest traces of life, tiny chemical ghosts locked in stone. When miners dig they cut through more than strata. They open time itself. The smell that rises from those shafts is sulphur and iron and sweat.

At night, fires burn in the yards and the ridges turn black against the sky. Smoke threads upward through eucalyptus leaves. A radio crackles somewhere, its signal fading in and out, drifting across the valleys until it becomes indistinguishable from the wind.

In the dark, the old and new traders share the same roads. The headlights of freight lorries have replaced the lanterns of Indian Ocean traders. The rhythm of movement does not change, only its engine.

Morning arrives with mist rising from the low ground, hanging in the gullies and on the fences. Dew beads on leaves planted for pulp, not shade. As the light strengthens, the outlines of farms emerge. A child walks to the road with a satchel. A tractor starts. A generator coughs to life.

In the late light the ridges turn blue. The pines along the slopes stand in ordered lines. Beyond them the rock faces glow red and the smoke from the mills curls white.

The escarpment has always been a frontier. Empires rose and fell on either side. Bapedi kings defended their valleys, Bokoni built stone villages. Prospectors came with their claims, administrators with their surveys. Each drew a grid across the surface; some grids failed in time. The land remains, resistant to design.

Somewhere near an old mine a farmer digs an irrigation trench. His spade strikes quartz and rings like a bell. He pauses, lights a cigarette, looks toward the horizon. The sky has the colour of old brass. The moment holds still, suspended between breath and work. Then he bends again to the task.

These hills attract people who live between categories. Runaways, fortune seekers, mystics, engineers, teachers who have learned patience from stone. Their stories are small but exact. Together they make a geography of persistence.

The sea lies far to the east, but its influence reaches here. Rain arrives heavy and slow, smelling faintly of salt. The soil darkens and the rivers swell. For a day or two they celebrate their own power, then the water subsides and the roads shine.

To move through Mpumalanga is to walk through different layers of time. You can travel from rocks older than life to fields sown last week in the space of an hour. The tension between what endures and what alters gives the place its character. New towns rise beside abandoned diggings. Wind carries seeds into the ruins.

Evening descends quickly. The mountains pool what light remains. Roads empty, fires sputter in the distance. The air smells of wood smoke and maize meal, eucalyptus and tobacco. Tyres crackle on gravel, laughter carries across a yard. The world settles into its slow night rhythm. The mountains maintain their hooded vigil while the people give it form.

There is a story that when we travel from the highveld and reach the escarpment, the lowveld stretches away like an ocean. Early in the morning the land looks like the skin of a lizard. The air shivers with heat and insect sound, the breath of the land is the hum of labour.

To stand here is to feel part of that continuity. The road bends, dust lifts, the smell of iron and pine mixes in the air. A crow circles once and calls. The pattern of *Mapalakata* endures. You can trace it in the rhythm of trucks, in the swing of a door, in the footpaths that curve through grass toward the next valley. Signifying travellers, a movement of lives through space, the quiet insistence of people making their way across a land that has stillness but is never still.

Desmond Latham

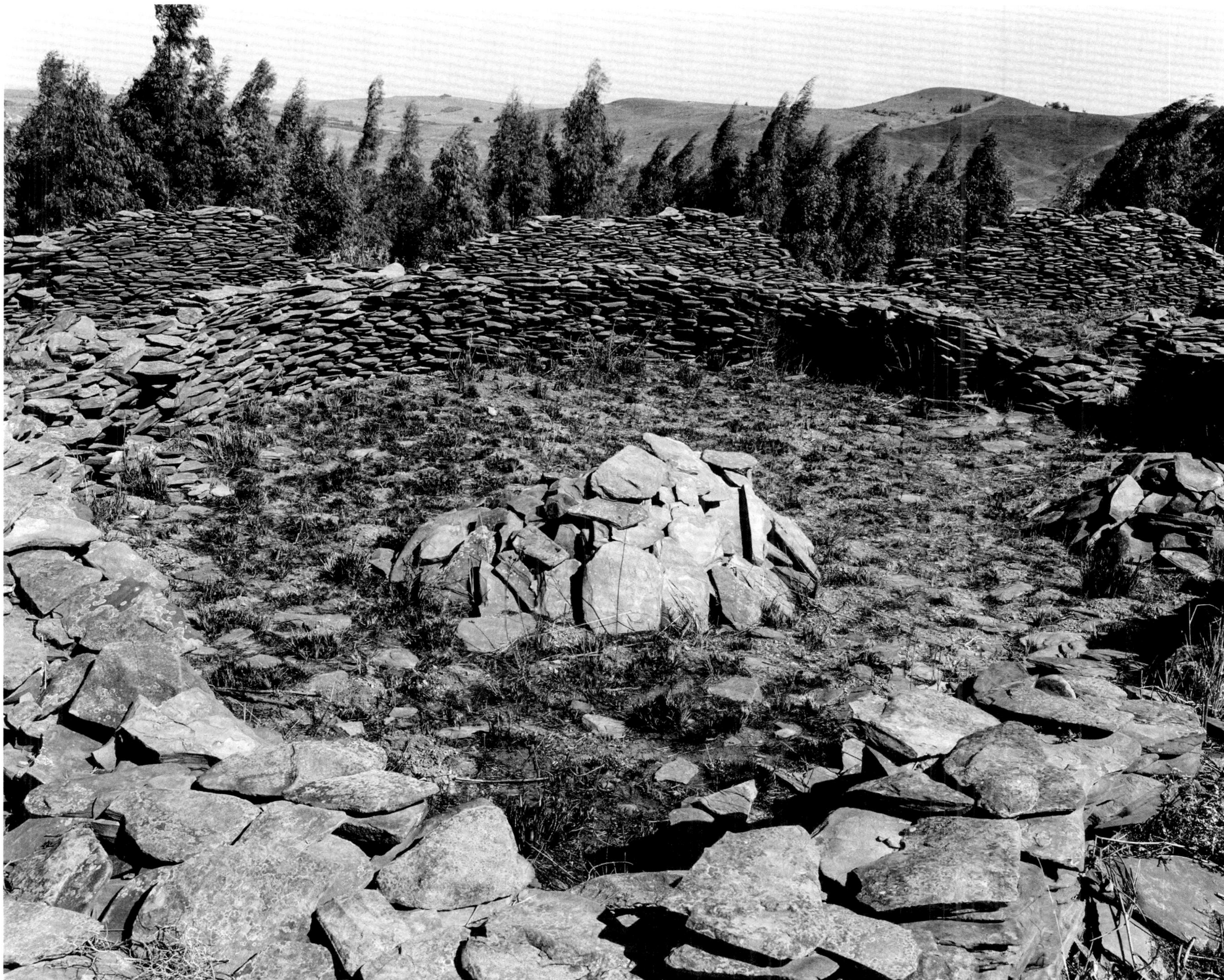

Mapalakata is an extinct word recorded in oral traditions of the area meaning 'visitors'—which was used to describe foreign traders and prospectors who moved through Southern Africa long before the time of contemporary European colonisation.

This book is dedicated to my grandparents, Rosemary and Norman, who carved the fullest of lives through unwavering persistence.

Thank you to the countless people who have been involved in helping to realise this project. Most importantly, I am grateful to the subjects of the portraits contained within this book and all the others I met along the way. You have all helped me get a little bit closer to understanding the nuances of place in our beautiful country.

Thank you Andrea Botha, Jacqueline Brits, Erick Maxwell Mondlane, Tebogo Mankge and Marycate Masilela for your hospitality and support during my many visits, and for showing me your worlds.

Thank you Desmond Latham and Lidudumalingani for understanding and articulating these themes with such clarity. To Alex Schneideman, Rabia Kader and Kerfi Sarkari for your technical precision with the film, prints and scans. To David Hill for your encouragement in the development of this work.

To Stuart Smith for your thoughtful guidance in the editing and designing of this book. I am also deeply grateful to the entire team at GOST Books, including Justine Hucker, Claudia Paladini, Gemma Gerhard and Katie Clifford for your help in bringing it to life.

Thank you to my family, peers and mentors—without you my way of seeing would not be the same. In particular thank you to Federica Angelucci, Eve Lyons, Pieter Hugo, Greg Halpern, Max Pinckers and Paul Schiek for your input in shaping this work over the years.

Finally thank you to my wife, Sarah, for inspiring, guiding and supporting my ideas—without you they would have no anchor.

Mapalakata
First published in 2026
by GOST Books, London

info@gostbooks.com
gostbooks.com

Edited and designed by GOST:
Katie Clifford, Gemma Gerhard, Justine Hucker, Allon Kaye, Nicola Jeffs, Claudia Paladini, Ana Rocha, Gabriela Szczypa

Printed in Italy by Grafiche Antiga

British Library cataloguing-in-publication data.
A catalogue record of this book is available from the British Library.

ISBN 978-1-80598-029-2